RACE
to
JESUS

RACE

to

JESUS

THE TIME IS **NOW**
TO WALK AS ONE

DR. CLARENCE HILL, JR.

DreamClock.org
RaceToJesus.com

Manufactured in the United States of America
10 9 8 7 6 5 4 3 2 1

ISBN-13: 979-8985625509

Table of Contents

Introduction

Do What Jesus Did

For many people, conversations around race awaken pain, division, and misunderstanding. There have been so many bitter conversations about the topic, that hopelessness has caused many to feel like there is no point in even trying to bridge divides.

I want to encourage you to not give up hope. I want to share with you how Jesus models for us tangible ways to overcome seemingly impossible cultural divides. We should not give up hope because over and over in the Scriptures we see evidence that it is God's heart expressed through Jesus that his followers be one. If this is his desire, his grace and wisdom are available to show us the way.

We can take comfort in the fact that we don't need to make up new ways to overcome divisions because Jesus offers a living example. The way that he, as a Jew, interacted with and spoke about Samaritans, the despised "other" to the Jews, shows us plenty of practical things we can do to follow in his footsteps in this area and show the world his heart concerning this topic.

If you have never studied the peculiar ways that Jesus included Samaritans as heroes in his stories, intentionally went through their towns, and engaged with them even though it was socially incorrect, you may be surprised by how applicable his words and solutions are for us today. But since Jesus is the same yesterday and today and forever, we can be assured that just as his life and teachings were relevant then, they are also relevant now.

These solutions work

Relief, hope, joy, compassion, willingness, and even excitement are feelings expressed by people who have heard the principles shared in this book. They've been shared in gatherings as part of the StrongerTogether.global movement and they are the Biblical version of the Dream Clock series, a step-by-step, hour-by-hour training that is simplifying and clarifying the path to tomorrow in the challenging conversation on race. These bridge-building principles have been shared across the United States in universities, schools, corporations, media outlets, government agencies, faith groups, and other compassion movements and honored in Washington, DC. The Dream Clock was featured twelve consecutive weeks in Oklahoma's largest newspaper, launching on the front page of the Sunday paper during the George Floyd crisis in 2020.

After a presentation of these ideas to a group of leaders in Austin, Texas, one well-respected African American pastor declared, "It is the best teaching on bridging the racial divide that I have ever heard." He went on to say, "I have been engaged in matters of racial reconciliation since the '90s. I have not only read books and attended seminars, but I have forged partnerships. I've sought to do the work. However, the racial tension, the cultural divide that we have experienced across the last couple of years left me discouraged, left me exhausted. But my hope has been restored. It re-introduced me to empathy. It has given me a better way of seeing our differences—a healthier way of moving toward my brothers and sisters in Christ. I've got my energy back."

I cannot take credit for these ideas. I must give credit where it is due. Jesus gets the credit. He taught and modeled these truths and calls us to follow his ways. Regarding issues of race, we can ask:

- Did Jesus say anything about how to handle racial challenges?
- Are there any examples from his life that will help us discover how to respond better?

The answers are yes and yes! There are many brilliant things Jesus did in response to the Jewish-Samaritan divide of his day that deserve closer inspection and greater implementation.

Jesus lived in a day of open, normalized, and expected ethnic division between Jews and Samaritans. When we discover his amazing responses and intentional strategies, we realize:

- Why our societies have been stuck in division
- Why some of our race conversations have fallen short
- Why discouragement is so common among unity proponents
- How everyone can do their part to make things better

Unity is a core desire of God, as evidenced in John 17:21 when Jesus says "I pray that they will all be one, just as you and I are one—as you are in me, Father, and I am in you. And may they be in us so that the world will believe you sent me."

Anyone who has made a concerted effort to reach for healing between ethnic groups knows that it can be challenging. There is a gap yet to be closed between the desire of Jesus's heart and our reality.

Race to Jesus is meant to bridge that distance and show us ways back to the desire of Jesus's and God the Father's heart for us to be one. The chapters provide a map to a future where an individual, family, team, school, church, organization, or city can become shining lights that lead us to a better tomorrow.

This journey is a mountain

The journey toward racial harmony is viewed by some like a long road trip. The idea is that if we just stay on the road, we will get there eventually. Keep gas in the tank, don't give up, and a better tomorrow will be just over the horizon.

I believe this picture falls short. The journey toward racial harmony is more than a long road trip. It is more like climbing a mountain. Highways have virtual maps, with clear destinations, estimated times of arrival, and even warnings about traffic and road conditions. A mountain, on the other hand, may have been mapped, but the question is more about what is on the inside of the climber than what is on the map. A driver will reach the destination on a highway if they just stay on the road. A mountain, however, will challenge the climber's desire and require more and more resolve the closer they get to the summit.

In Dr. Martin Luther King Jr.'s last message before his assassination, he said that he had been to the mountaintop. It seems telling that he used a mountain as the best picture to describe his life's journey toward racial harmony.

One of the reasons there is so much disappointment and anger around the topic of race is because we think the road to tomorrow is a clear and obvious highway. The signs on the highway that are pointing us toward loving one another better seem like they are just being ignored. We find it hard to comprehend why racial issues can't be easily addressed and why others don't see the way we see.

This is because the journey is not a highway; it's a mountain. An individual, a family, a church, a community or a nation that summits this mountain and rises above offense, partiality, greed, and self-interest will gain the world's attention. Perhaps that is why Jesus said the world would know who he was if his people (from every nation, or *ethnos*, or ethnic group) were one. Being one is not what usually happens in the nations of the world. It would definitely take Heaven and transformed hearts to produce something better!

History shows us that pain connected to ethnic division is more than a matter of uncomfortable and tense relationships. Unchecked division and bitterness can get worse and even deadly. It has led to genocide, wars, slavery, broken treaties, and generational pain. It has been a stumbling block to societies trying to move beyond painful memories.

Nation after nation has fallen short of producing harmony between ethnic groups. Division is a danger to any society and does not heal on its own. The United States has seen 400 years of tensions between Blacks and Whites producing the Civil War, lynchings, the rise of the Klan, Jim Crow Laws and what seems to be a never-ending stalemate between yesterday and tomorrow. Nazi Germany produced the Holocaust, where millions of Jews were murdered, and many others were displaced. South Africa created apartheid and a division between the whites, blacks, and browns that left economic disparities with Black townships of gross poverty literal steps away from prosperous white communities.

Ethnic division is also not just about blacks and whites. Rwanda showed us that ethnic division can go beyond skin color in the 1994 genocidal rampage of the Hutus against the Tutsis where 800,000 neighbors were slaughtered in 90 days. A deeper look shows Belgian colonists creating this division by claiming Tutsis were closer to Europeans than Hutus and held racial superiority. Tutsis were identified by their physical traits. This smaller percentage of Rwandans were treated as the upper class and Hutus were treated as the lower working class, with less opportunity based solely on ethnicity and not skill or character. Once again, hatred and death were the results.

Their division was man-made. These Rwandans actually had to carry racial identity cards to distinguish between Hutus and Tutsis. Caste systems, and divides between the haves and the have nots, prevail in the Middle East, India, other Asian countries and throughout the world.

There are too many examples of the pain and potential of division from all over the world to name them all. "Heaven on earth" is never the result of beliefs toward others that do not reflect the heart of God. Division and failure to conquer this mountain is ultimately bad for us all.

Scaling this mountain is more than a nice option to casually try. It is our responsibility to seek to make things better for those who will come after us by reflecting God's heart towards other ethnic groups regardless of the price. Division is not something to sit around and be okay with. Reading about such moments in history should break our hearts.

We aren't the first to care about racial harmony. Many before us have worked to make things better. They have led calls for repentance, held unity services, erected memorials, fought for just laws, penned hidden and overlooked history, and advanced initiatives to include stories that help us respect the sacrifices, challenges, and contributions of other ethnic groups. But we still wonder what else is needed to help us reach tomorrow

Jesus is our ultimate guide

To climb this mountain toward racial harmony, we need more than a map. We need a guide who has already made it to the summit and is willing to lead us there. Climbing a great mountain is no small feat. Just as Mount Everest and Mount Kilimanjaro are two of the world's greatest mountains to climb, the ideal of racial harmony is a mountain that presents one of history's greatest challenges.

Even the Apostle Peter stumbled in his attitude and behavior toward brand-new believers who were outside his ethnic group (see Galatians 2:11-14). One of the first internal challenges in the church, mentioned in Acts 6, was a dispute between how Hebrew widows were being treated better than Greek widows. So, we see that racial issues are nothing new and are a familiar human fault. Yet they still have no place in God's Kingdom.

For this challenge, we need a guide, and not just any guide, but a capable one. Trying to conquer a great mountain without a successful guide is foolish and perhaps even dangerous. If you research great mountains, you can find lists of people who died trying to reach the summit. We don't want to add to the number of those who tried and failed. Life is too short to "run aimlessly" or "fight like one who is beating the wind" (1 Corinthians 9:26). Division and racial issues are a great mountain, but Jesus conquered it. This book is an opportunity to learn from a guide, Jesus, who knows how to conquer the mountain of division.

Jesus knows how to bridge the relationship gap. He is the most qualified because he healed the greatest breach, which was our broken relationship with God. Jesus also knows how to change the story of ethnic division. Being born a Jew, he demonstrated what it meant to reject cultural division and relate to those his own people hated and despised, which were the Samaritans in his day.

Jesus lives on the summit. His character, his teachings, and the life he modeled produce the wisest and most effective response to ethnic division. These are more than just biblical ideas that relate well to the race topic. They are his direct responses to the ethnic division he saw firsthand between Jews and Samaritans during his life on earth. In

Race to Jesus, we will:

- Locate where we are on the path to bridging divides
- Get a sense of where others are, so we have realistic expectations and an idea of how best to relate Find clear direction on how to be a part—or become a more effective part—of the fulfillment of Jesus's prayer that we might "all be one"

You may not have much hope when it comes to the race conversation. You may believe that race relations are as good as they are going to get this side of heaven. Either way, we are still called to live like Jesus, and that is what this book is about.

I believe we can make a difference in our worlds. I don't believe we are called to be a part of the bitterness and envy, nor are we to get entangled in the things of this world in a way that takes us off our mission to love all our neighbors and share the Good News of God's Kingdom. The summit of this mountain is high and challenging only because we have fallen so far from reflecting God's love and character to our neighbors. We can do better. By God's grace, we will do better.

These ideas work. We have seen plenty examples of how people respond to race. Now, let's discover how Jesus responded. Proverbs 13:10 in the Amplified Bible says, "Through pride and presumption come nothing but strife. But [skillful and godly] wisdom is with those who welcome [well-advised] counsel."

We've had enough strife. Let's consider what wisdom Jesus had concerning overcoming ethnic division. Is it possible that Jesus was born into a time of ethnic division between Jews and Samaritans so we could have a clear example of how to respond and make a difference? In John 17:20-23, we see Jesus praying about his people being one three times! This is what Jesus wanted. If Jesus wants us to be one, then I want us to be one.

Our transformation begins with us aligning our desires to the desires of Jesus. The first step is to soften our hearts towards one another by praying like Jesus prayed. Pray that we would be one. In fact, we can pray right now: "Father, we pray that we all might be one just like it says in John 17:21. Show us how to do our part so that your plans will become our reality. Amen." If you prayed that prayer sincerely from the heart, get ready to make a greater difference than ever and discover what race meant to Jesus.

Chapter 1

Jesus Understood His Palace | Understand Your Palace

1 o'clock

"The woman was surprised, for Jews refuse to have anything to do with Samaritans. She said to Jesus, 'You are a Jew, and I am a Samaritan woman. Why are you asking me for a drink?'" John 4:9

Comfortable and Familiar - The campus cafeteria was full and noisy. You could hear laughter and lots of chatter. Only a few tables had any seats available. There were three major groups of people. The left side of the cafeteria was the Hispanic and Latino section. The main seating area in the middle was dominated by Whites. Blacks were in a smaller section on the right side of the room.

These students knew one another, shared classes together, were on teams together, and lived on the same dorm floors, but they ate with "their own." There were no signs in the cafeteria that demanded people to sit with their ethnic group. The cafeteria had open seating. Was everyone racist, or were they doing what was familiar?

Jesus knew his palace

In Jesus's day, the lines between ethnic groups were also clear. In fact, the tensions between Jews and Samaritans were so bad that even a Jewish man thirsty and weary from travel normally would not ask for help from a Samaritan. But Jesus didn't abide by "normal" social laws.

Jesus had the first 30 years of his life to observe, question, pray, and get answers about the Jewish world. In Luke 2:41-52, we find a brief glimpse of 12-year-old Jesus choosing to spend his time in the synagogue inquiring about the Scriptures and the will of his Father. He saw how Jews treated others. He saw their prejudices and double standards. He was people watching and learning from others' mistakes like King Solomon often did, as we see when we read Proverbs. He also saw the things that were good. By the time he started his ministry at age 30, he had taken plenty of time to seek the Scriptures and pray about what it meant to love others.

Jesus knew the pride and pitfalls of his people group, the Jews. Every ethnic group has them. He knew their strengths and failures. He knew their right and wrong interpretations of Scripture. He knew the differences between how they served God and what their heavenly Father actually wanted.

Jesus also knew of the problematic and hypocritical postures of the Jewish religious leaders, who often loved attention, money, and the praise of men more than God (see Matthew 23). These leaders had the platform and touted the Scriptures, but their hearts were focused on the wrong things. They did not represent the Father in their love toward others and therefore did not lead the people to respond to others in love, especially not towards Samaritans.

I refer to Jesus' knowledge of the Jews and the world he grew up in as knowing and understanding his palace. We all have palace relationships. A palace has thick walls, controlled entry, and the highest levels of comfort and security. In the context of relationships, I am referring to the people or community with whom we are most familiar, the most confident and the most comfortable. We know one another's social cues and have a higher confidence in communicating with them. Unless we train ourselves differently, we will generally behave and respond to others and to life just like this group.

The palace forms our likes, dislikes, perspectives, and expectations. Because of the history of America, most people's palace of relationships is first among their ethnic group and second among their wealth or socioeconomic class. For others, their palace is simply those with whom they have a shared background or shared experiences.

Out of all the people on earth, your palace is the people group who could most likely finish your sentences and understand your stories and jokes without a lot of explanation. Around them, we feel confident that they will understand our intent and meaning when we communicate. Around them, we know we connect or have a level entrance (even with perfect strangers). We can even feel a sense of belonging and like we fit.

Jesus was born a Jew, so the Jewish community would be considered his palace community. We understand that Jesus was born of a virgin and his Father is God, but Joseph, Mary, and the Jews were his earthly, ethnic community. He was raised as a Jew, attended their festivals, followed their customs, and became familiar with their social expectations. He heard their unfiltered, backroom conversations. He knew what they generally liked and disliked and who they actually liked and disliked. He could tell you all about a year in the life of a Jew by experience.

The Jews were not the only community Jesus encountered, but they were his primary earthly community. He also lived part of his childhood in Egypt and crossed paths with the occupying armies of Rome. He met Greeks and travelers from around the world. He had experiences with other ethnic groups but would have been keenly aware of the main ethnic group the Jews hated and despised, which were the Samaritans.

Jesus was born to fulfill the prophecies given to the Jews. He was clear about his assignment. He knew that his Jewish world did not reflect God's heart in everything, yet he displayed God's heart in every situation. He knew when not to go along with the behavior of his people and his culture. Do you know when to refuse to agree with your palace community? His earthly palace world was Jewish, but he lived by the code of his Father in heaven, and we are called to do the same.

"Us" and "them"

In John 4:7-9, we see Jesus encountering a Samaritan woman at a well. The ethnic lines of division clearly marked the "us" and the "them." The us-es were the Jews. The thems were the Samaritans. Jews seemed to not only justify their hatred of Samaritans but did so as though they were expressing a *holy* posture of indignation toward them. The Samaritans had intermarried with non-Jews, changed the location of the temple, and had the audacity to defend their place as the proper site for worship. It seemed right to them that hating them and rejecting was the right response. These opinions are hinted at when Jesus encounters this Samaritan woman alone at a well.

In John 4, we find Jesus weary from a long journey. He was tired and had sent his disciples into this Samaritan village to buy food. He sat down by a well without anything to use to draw water. When a Samaritan woman came, he asked her for a drink. She was shocked and said, "You are a Jew, and I am a Samaritan woman. Why are you asking me for a drink?" (John 4:9b).

What a telling response! The division between their communities was so strong that even though Jesus was tired and thirsty, the woman still did not expect him, a Jewish man, to say anything to her because that would be breaking social laws.

Most Jews chose to avoid going through Samaria at all costs. Some Jews even considered Samaritan water unclean (apparently, they had separate water fountains back then too). Our human behaviors with regard to division and the "other" are old and repeat for generations until someone chooses to behave differently.

Jesus knew she wouldn't expect him to speak. Jesus knew his palace world had a real history of hating and despising her palace community of Samaritans. If Jesus thought like a normal Jew, the woman would have received the treatment she expected—no communication, or even hostility.

Jesus, however, took the opportunity to show something better. He broke with the social laws of the Jews. He applied the Second Commandment to love his neighbor as himself, even when the messages and sermons he heard growing up found a way to justify treating Samaritans as invisible or less than human. He treated her the way heaven would. She was seen, acknowledged, and spoken to in the same way that he would have respected a Jewish woman or someone else from his palace community.

Understand the contributions and blind spots of your palace

Palace relationships are not evil, but they can become a dangerous echo chamber, where we only hear opinions that reinforce our own. Jesus was able to grow up in Jewish culture without being formed by Jewish culture. He didn't ignore or overlook behaviors that didn't match the heart of the Scriptures.

Jesus had victory over his culture like it says in Romans 12:2: "Don't copy the behavior and customs of this world, but let God transform you into a new person by changing the way you think. Then you will learn to know God's will for you, which is good and pleasing and perfect."

It was good, pleasing, and perfect for Jesus not to behave like those in his palace community. It was good, pleasing, and perfect for Jesus to treat a Samaritan (or them) with the same dignity he would a Jew. To Jesus, if another Jew didn't like him interacting with a Samaritan woman as he would a Jew, that was their problem. Jesus lived to please the Father, not his palace community (John 8:29).

Jesus had several encounters with the mind-molders of his day, who were the Pharisees and the scribes. These religious leaders taught the people how to think. They had the same Old Testament Scriptures that we have today but consistently landed on different viewpoints than Jesus did. Jesus called them blind leaders of the blind (Matthew 15:14).

When we read about the Pharisees praying long public prayers, seeking to be seen on street corners, loving money, loving praise, and loving to sit in the best seats in the room, we wonder how they could be so blind and not see their sin. The answer is simple: the same way that we don't see our sin. Somewhere in Jewish history the Pharisees behavior was accepted as normal and was not repented of.

We all have blind spots, areas of sin in our lives that we either can't see or choose not to see. It can be easy to point fingers at leaders, authorities, or others to call out their faults but not recognize our own.

John 9 says that the only people who will receive the gift of being able to see (beyond the norms of their palace cultures and social expectations) are those who first are willing to confess their own blindness. These behaviors we learn in our palace are almost as second nature as breathing. The first challenge to not conform to the negative and unbiblical behaviors of our palace communities is to humbly confess that we have blind spots. God's grace comes to those who humble themselves according to James 4:6.

We also must fight against worshipping the biggest idol we all face: ourselves. As soon as we prosper, we love to claim how smart and strong we are instead of how merciful and gracious God is. This was the warning to the Israelites after they survived the wilderness and were entering the promised land (Deuteronomy 8).

Jesus understood that the Jews were chosen because God was good, not because the Jews were. This meant that the same mercy the Samaritans seemed to obviously need, the Jews needed too. Only through humility could Jesus discover this truth while being raised in the lineage of King David and in the land of the people chosen by God.

Reflect Jesus, not the palace

Different ethnic groups are great at different things, sometimes by necessity because of where they live. But the Bible refuses to place people as anything more than (or less than) the children of Adam who need forgiveness for sin, regardless of their ethnic group, skin color, or wealth class. We must be careful of the blinding power that comes from the moral, monetary, or positional strength we find in our own ethnic groups.

Those who know they have blind spots will discover how to love others as Jesus did. They will be aware of the tendencies of those from their own palace worlds. They will be aware of how easy it is to love the familiar and stay in palace spaces among palace relationships. They will be aware of their own tendency to build a lifestyle where they have the least interactions with "them."

Having a palace is less of a character defect; it's human nature. We all have a palace community. When events come on the news or decisions are made, we can usually guess what the majority of our palace community is thinking. If we don't renew our minds through prayer and the Word of God, we could easily agree with wrong responses or pick up offenses. Instead, we are called to be intentional in asking: How would Jesus respond?

I don't want to respond to issues of race like many of the preachers in the American South who refused to reject slavery because it was the cultural norm and because their economy and salaries depended on the evil system. I also don't want to become embittered at mistreatment and offenses to the point where I refuse to believe and pray for God's children to be one. I don't want to carry resentment toward those who couldn't care less about those I care about. Blindness is blindness, and we are called to see.

Not only are we called to see, but we are called to be salt and light in the world. We are called to engage with those outside our palace worlds. We are called to interact with other ethnic groups with the same grace that we offer our own. We are called to be aware of moments when we are tempted to avoid spaces and interactions with others because they make us uncomfortable.

Acknowledging our palaces is the starting place to discover how to love others well. Until we are trained to behave like Jesus, we are likely reflecting the communities that formed us and building relationships around things that are familiar. Once we recognize our tendency to reflect our palace communities more than the heart of Jesus, we can then acknowledge our blind spots, confess our shortcomings, and ask God to change our hearts and actions.

Chapter 2

Jesus Rejected Social Walls | Reject Social Walls

2 o'clock

"Soon a Samaritan woman came to draw water, and Jesus said to her, 'Please give me a drink.'" John 4:7

Seen and Welcomed - Daisy finally worked up the nerve to check out some of the famous (and expensive) stores in Beverly Hills on Rodeo Drive. She was nervous because she knew she couldn't afford anything in them. She determined to just slip in and out without taking up anyone's time.

Daisy believed that these retail workers were likely trained to recognize who had money and who did not. She couldn't get this irritating thought out of her head, and it was ruining her mood. As soon as she stepped into the store, a warm and genuine welcome came from behind the counter, "Good morning! Take your time and let me know if I can be of assistance."

In one moment, Daisy's concerns were no more. What a difference a greeting makes!

Jesus knew the power of kindness

Jesus rejected cultural expectations, not people. He intentionally engaged with people outside of his ethnic group, regardless of what was socially acceptable. As he observed the behavior of his Jewish community and others, he knew what could immediately make a difference between these divided ethnic groups. Jesus actually paid attention to how people greeted one another. He noticed how his fellow Jews tended to ignore or give little attention to those who weren't part of their ethnic group.

Jesus was raised around Jews and knew what they thought about Samaritans. That's why when he engaged the woman at the well in John 4, she was shocked. Jesus took the initiative to start a conversation and engage with her. Jews never said anything positive about Samaritans. If Jews came to a Samaritan village, they would go around it rather than through it. Just like most of us today have certain streets and neighborhoods we don't go through.

Not only did Jesus reject social walls by addressing the Samaritan woman, but he even said "please." Rather than treating her scornfully, or like someone who was below him, he asked her kindly for a drink. Later, he addressed her as "dear woman." He shows us that the way we acknowledge and speak to people matters. How do you engage other ethnic groups? In what tone do you engage people that are serving you or who seem to have less wealth?

Jesus knew his Jewish brothers and sisters could be self-righteous and that they couldn't stand Samaritans. Since he fulfilled his earthly ministry in a day that had racial issues too, he knew the challenge we would face to greet with kindness those outside our palace communities. What a brilliant and disarming first step toward spreading the love of God and opening hearts!

Beware of showing partiality

The Apostle James asks, "My dear brothers and sisters, how can you claim to have faith in our glorious Lord Jesus Christ if you favor some people over others?" (James 2:1). But the love of God is greater than comfortable, mutually beneficial relationships. The proof that the great love of Jesus dwells in us is most shown by how we love and engage those outside our palace walls.

In Matthew 5:46-47, Jesus said, "If you love only those who love you, what reward is there for that? Even corrupt tax collectors do that much. If you are kind only to your friends, how are you different from anyone else? Even pagans do that." If we only engage our palace ethnic group and wealth class, we are not proving that the love in us is any greater than what the world has.

Think about how thick the walls of your palace are or how homogeneous are the people with whom you spend most of your time. Remember that in the United States and many other countries the main dividers historically are first ethnicity and then wealth class—and in a rising number of situations, politics. This is where the pain of division is greatest.

We may be known as the kindest and most loving person to our friends, coworkers, and fellow church members, but in that case, Jesus says we are doing no more than what unbelievers do with their friends. Our light shines when we love those who do not love us back and we greet those who would never expect us to take the time to speak to them, learn their names, or show them kindness. This is a sobering truth. Jesus is saying that our love shows no proof of being from Heaven as long as we are just loving others who love us back. This means we can make the wall of fame among our palace friends and our palace community and be doing no more than what people do who don't know God.

How do you see and engage other ethnic groups? How do you see and engage other wealth classes? Do you have a positive image of them? Does it even cross your mind to smile, say hello or show kindness? Our behavior towards others has a lot to do with how we see them.

Our palace spaces are typically not great places to gain a positive image of those outside of our communities. The things that are spoken about others in our palace communities very often have a negative tone or produce a negative image of them. Palaces are erected to preserve the good things about our heritage not theirs. We put our accomplishments on the walls of our palace. We boast of our great works and positive deeds in our palaces. We minimize the negative and promote what we believe is good. This is typical palace behavior.

Some may say they didn't learn negative images of other groups, but maybe there was an absence of images that included other groups at all, so your community rarely saw other groups celebrated in any way in songs, images, history books and stories. Realizing that our palaces have probably not prepared us to have great relationships with outsiders can help us overcome our blind spots too.

Maybe you think this isn't an issue for you because you smile at and are kind to everybody. But think about how long you converse with people who are not in the same ethnic or wealth group as you? Is it longer for those in your same palace community? Think about who the non-palace individuals are around you and how many of them you cross paths with daily. How do you engage them?

Think about who your us-es and thems are. Think about those who work in or around your palace world. How do you engage those non-palace people who work or do life in your palace spaces?

Our opportunities to interact vary depending on how many are in our daily worlds and the routes we travel on a weekly basis. Typically, we have well-worn palace routes. We have our palace grocery store, gas station, job, and hangout place. If we just live by default, we gravitate toward spaces that are familiar and comfortable to us.

I am not saying someone is an evil or bad person if they want to hang out with people in their us group. It's human nature to dwell in places where we feel safe, seen, and known, where we can rest. We all want someone to be able to look at us across the room and get what we're talking about or share in a private joke. We love intimate relationships. So, of course, we're not going to naturally choose to enter a place we feel is hostile toward us. We're going to be drawn instead to the comfort of our palace.

However, to follow Jesus means that we do his will, even when it's uncomfortable or unfamiliar. We choose to be intentional to live on mission, the mission that aligns with the Father's heart and that follows Jesus's example. The only reason we will intentionally go beyond our palace comfort is if we remember that we are on assignment to follow Jesus.

Love your neighbor as yourself

Jesus goes right to the heart when he says, "If you are kind only to your friends, how are you different from anyone else?" He knows that how we behave toward the outsider, the "them," is indicative of the true state of our hearts. If we go around or speak harshly to an outsider, we are not exhibiting the Father's heart.

Ignoring someone is no better, since it only shows that we don't acknowledge that they exist or that they are, in essence, dead to us. We don't hate them. We don't love them. We don't want their good, nor their bad. We are just indifferent. Indifference is not what Jesus desires of us. He wants our love to be greater than the world's.

Many businesses have discovered that greeting people with kindness, learning their names, and being excited about serving them, makes them want to come back.

"How may I serve you?"

"May I have a name for this order?"

"My pleasure!"

These simple one-liners help customers know they are seen, welcome, and appreciated. The opposite is true when they enter a store and feel like they are in the way or making someone's day harder and no one wants to help them.

Think about heaven. It's a big invitation to us all through Jesus Christ, and according to Luke 15, there is a huge celebration the minute anyone accepts the invitation.

Remember the parable of the one lost sheep out of ninety-nine that was pursued and found, Luke 15:7 says, "I say to you that likewise there will be more joy in heaven over one sinner who repents than over ninety-nine just persons who need no repentance.

Remember the parable of the lost coin, Luke 15:10 says, "Likewise, I say to you, there is joy in the presence of the angels of God over one sinner who repents."

Remember the story of the prodigal son, Luke 15:22-23 says, "But the father said to his servants, 'Bring out the best robe and put it on him, and put a ring on his hand and sandals on his feet. And bring the fatted calf here and kill it, and let us eat and be merry; for this my son was dead and is alive again; he was lost and is found.' And they began to be merry."

I love heaven's culture!

Jesus teaches us the laws of the culture of heaven. He shows us the positive power of greeting and the negative power of ignoring. When we engage warmly with someone who has a deep-rooted belief that we or "our kind" don't like them, it makes them think twice. It can make a hardened hearts begin to soften and reconsider. When we smile at them and want to know their name, we are helping to heal negative, preconceived notions. We make more room for the love of God to prevail over bitterness and hatred.

You might be at the grocery store just trying to buy some groceries. You aren't trying to run for office, so you're not trying to greet everybody on the way into the store. But when you're putting Jesus first, you enter that space with a high value for the opportunities you will have to greet and show kindness to those outside of your palace world. You are aware of how when you ignore a person from outside your group, you may be reinforcing every negative thing they thought about your palace group.

Again, that doesn't mean you have to wave at every single person going up and down the street, but remember how Jesus said that we have a love within us that is greater than what is in the world. How can we share that greater love in everyday life? By greeting people and showing kindness to those who are outside of our palace communities. What a powerful impact followers of Jesus can have on any and every space we enter! All we have to do is smile, show kindness, and refuse to be focused on ourselves all day.

It doesn't matter if they don't smile back.

It doesn't matter if it is uncomfortable, or you don't feel cool doing it.

It doesn't matter if they don't say thank you.

It doesn't matter if they mock you for being kind.

This is how we can make a difference in our everyday lives and be more like Jesus. So, there's power in greeting people, and there's also power in ignoring people. One of the first steps to make a difference and tear down walls of division is to simply see people, especially those outside our palace relationships, and then engage them with grace and kindness as Jesus would. Break ungodly social laws and be kind anyway. This is what Jesus did when he met the Samaritan woman at the well and a whole city of Samaritans came to believe on Him for themselves.

Chapter 3

Jesus Stood Up for Others | Stand Up for Others

3 o'clock

> *"So he left Judea and returned to Galilee. He had to go through Samaria on the way. Eventually, he came to the Samaritan village of Sychar, near the field that Jacob gave to his son Joseph." John 4:3-5*

Supported and Defended - Two frustrated employees of an American corporation left their meeting with the highly paid contractors from India who were helping their team learn the latest technologies. The two longtime coworkers found a space where they thought no one was listening and poured out their grief and contempt at having to listen to their Indian accents and work with "outsiders."

Another employee overheard their conversation and recognized that their new foreign teammates would not be getting much support at succeeding in their roles. So, she used her influence with management to take on the role of onboarding all contractors, learn their expertise, and make sure their contribution to the company would not be blocked due to their ethnicity. She used her influence to stand up for others and benefit her organization.

Jesus defended those outside his palace

In order to further prepare the disciples to carry his message to the world, Jesus led his disciples into spaces with those outside their palace community. Though the cultural expectation was for Jews to avoid Samaritan towns and villages, Jesus purposefully led them through Samaritan spaces. This helped his disciples relate to others and helped expose some of the disciples' wrong attitudes (Luke 9:51-56).

Have you considered visiting spaces where you will have the opportunity to interact with people outside of your palace community? Perhaps you wondered why God led you to a certain job or city that put you around more of them. It could be your time to grow and to learn to love those who did not grow up in your palace community.

Luke 9:51 says, "As the time drew near for him to ascend to heaven, Jesus resolutely set out for Jerusalem. He sent messengers ahead to a Samaritan village to prepare for his arrival. But the people of the village did not welcome Jesus because he was on his way to Jerusalem. When James and John saw this, they said to Jesus, 'Lord, should we call down fire from heaven to burn them up?' But Jesus turned around and rebuked them."

Jesus rebuked them. He rebuked James and John for calling for a punishment for the Samaritans, realizing it was likely motivated by the fact that they were dealing with a group outside their palace community.

Though Jesus had been received in Samaritan villages before, he wasn't this time because they were offended that he was on his way to Jerusalem. However, rather than correct the Samaritans, Jesus corrected those in his palace community. There is a time to speak up in your palace communities and address conversations that are condescending towards others and not pleasing to God. This is what Jesus did. He did not just comply or go along with cultural animosity.

In us vs. them situations, judgments toward the thems are typically far harsher than judgments toward the us-es. When we read the gospels, we see several times where the Jews were trying to set up Jesus so they could stone him and more than one situation where they even picked up stones. Yet not one of those times did Jesus's disciples ask whether they should call down fire from heaven on them, even though their lives were being threatened. Instead, they let those offenses go.

In this passage, they were merely not given a place to stay, and they wanted to see the Samaritans burned with fire. Does that sound like justice? Is that impartial behavior from the men who would one day have their names on the foundations of the New Jerusalem (Revelation 21:14)? Don't be surprised that man's courts will typically find harsher sentences for them than us...no matter who the groups may be. Partiality is human nature. Justice is God's nature. The Bible says in Proverbs that God loves a just balance (Proverbs 11:1). This was not just judgment.

Palace partiality

In every case of division, there is one question that prevails: Who are the bad people? The answer is always "them." The us-es have good intentions; the thems have bad intentions. If one of us does something wrong, then you did not understand what they meant to do, or they made a mistake. If one of them does something wrong, it proves who they are, how bad they are, and that what we've been saying about them in our palace, behind closed doors and in some cases in public, is true. This us-them mentality is so easy to fall into, but it is not pleasing to God.

King David showed partiality when he thought the story of the man who took the poor man's sheep was someone else, the judgment was harsh. But later, when he found out that the story was about him, he thought differently (2 Samuel 12).

This way of thinking can also be subtle. Most followers of Jesus would probably claim to not think this way. They may have even quoted these popular one-liners: "I'm colorblind," "I love everybody," "I treat everybody the same," and "There's only one race, the human race." Those whose faith is in Jesus know enough about his message of love and forgiveness to try to say the right thing and may even be

100 percent sincere (in their hearts) when they say it.

It's easy, however, to claim love from a distance. It's easy to spend most of our time in the safety of our palace communities and make great declarations of love. But Jesus knows us better than we know ourselves. He knows we have some attitudes and animosities toward others that may be so subtle that we don't even believe we have them. He knows that these deeper heart attitudes often only come out when we "rub shoulders" or interact with *them*.Partiality is something that requires a work of God to remove from our hearts. One of the biggest blind spots we have is that we treat those outside our palace communities in harsher ways than we treat those inside. We so easily make conclusions and generalizations of character about them from inside the safety of our palace worlds.

Defend the outsider

It is natural for us to defend our palace community when they are not around. We will defend perfect strangers who look like us or represent our palace communities. It is even natural to overlook the faults of those in our palace communities and highlight the faults of those outside our palace communities.

We have to be intentional if we are to avoid falling into negative palace conversations. Consider the spaces where you remain silent when you hear condescending racial slurs. How could you be proactive and speak up when those close to you are using terms that would be offensive to those outside our community?

Our palace worlds may have painted negative images of other groups, labeling them as weak and fearful or even evil, corrupt, and greedy. The way of division is to label *them* with non-human terms like devils, dogs, pigs, coons, or cockroaches. These terms dehumanize others made in the image of God. Look at any genocide or situation of oppression and slavery and somewhere along the way a dehumanizing label was used to identify that whole people group.

Jesus calls us by our names and may even give us new and more beautiful names to show us who we are. He calls Peter a rock. He calls James and John - sons of thunder. Darkness strips us of our glory and identity, demeans us, calls us beasts and seeks to make us less than God has called us to be. Man will call you out. Jesus calls us up.

Those negative and dehumanizing terms and ideas are repeated more commonly when "they" are not in the room. I call these palace conversations. Palace conversations can be dangerous because we are comfortable and know those around us understand us. We don't have to explain a lot and can cut to the chase. We often have more colorful words to explain our points when it is just us in the room because we are not so concerned about being misunderstood. We are less concerned about giving account for what we say or being caught saying those things. In fact, on the other side, we want our point to be made even more clearly with passion and feeling than with rhetoric and explanation. Maybe that is why James and John so freely asked Jesus about calling down fire from heaven to burn up the Samaritans. Perhaps, they felt that old, raw Jewish hatred. Perhaps, they felt their Jewishness being threatened by some Samaritans who would dare reject them. Perhaps they believed that these Samaritans needed to be put in their place.

Luke 9:51-56 shows us how Jesus responded to this negative palace conversation. Jesus rebuked them and their wrong attitudes! Notice there aren't any Samaritans around when Jesus rebuked James and John for their harshness. He confronts them privately, but he does confront them.

Who do you defend when they are not around or when their character is being misrepresented? Do you defend only those in your palace community? Or do you defend the thems also?

When Jesus was in a space with his palace community and they used derogatory terms and condescending language, Jesus did not just stay silent. He did not chuckle and say, "No, not a firestorm, just something light." He didn't make a joke or indicate that it was funny in the slightest.

Jesus defended outsiders when they were being spoken of in a condescending way and when negative images were being declared about them. The strength of Jesus's rebuke of the disciples matched the strength of their statements against the Samaritans. Jesus does not endorse negative palace conversations.

To break this natural human bent to believe the worst of other groups, Jesus intentionally took the disciples through spaces with Samaritans, so they could see Samaritans and their worlds beyond what they were taught in their palace communities. The us-them narrative demands that we determine who is bad. The Bible says that all have sinned and fallen short of the glory of God (Romans 3:23). Be aware when you start getting too comfortable around your palace group in a conversation so that you don't lower your standards and begin to demean others. Doing what Jesus did calls for courage when no one else will praise you for it.

We have all heard stories of hot mic fiascos where someone talked as they would behind closed doors but the microphone was on, so others got to hear what they really thought. If we practice talking about others and standing up for them in spaces where we will get no credit and may even suffer, then we will never have to worry about "accidentally" saying something about them when they are not around and then getting caught.

Drop your stones

Jesus will not side with those who hypocritically accuse others but refuse to face the sins, misjudgments, and weaknesses of themselves or their own palace communities. Think about the story of the woman caught in adultery. Men had lined up to stone her after claiming they had caught her in the act of adultery. Strangely, we never hear about the man. Jesus immediately recognized their hypocrisy, and in the wisdom of God told them that whoever was without sin should cast the first stone. They soon dropped their stones and left. It is now our time to drop our stones and be more like Jesus.

Jesus didn't justify the behavior of the adulterous woman, but in his kindness, as he does with all of us, he told her to go and sin no more. We are not treating others with love and grace because they have not sinned or because we ignore their wrongdoing. We love others because he first loved us.

We also are recognizing that our grace toward non-palace people shouldn't be less than our grace toward our palace community. Jesus does not endorse sinful behavior, but he also does not endorse hypocritical misinterpretations of the Word of God and gathering in palace conversations to condemn others while turning a blind eye to our own sins.

We often claim to love everyone the same, yet we live most of our lives in the comfort of our palace relationships where our true feelings can never be exposed. Sometimes we don't know our true feelings toward others until we are appalled at them for treating us the same way we have treated them. Before Jesus rebuked James and John, I wonder whether they were even aware of their feelings toward Samaritans or whether they simply had never considered that "loving your neighbor" meant loving Samaritans too.

Visit the communities of those outside your palace community. Discover their food, restaurants, stores, and celebrations. Put yourself in spaces where you are the minority in the room. Be in spaces where you can see them enjoying one another, enjoying their culture, and enjoying their relationships. Make opportunities for the bent images that were formed in your heart and mind in your palace to be challenged through real relationships by finding ways to be around those who are ethnically Samaritans to your palace community.

Stand up for others like Jesus did and be careful of the tone of your palace conversations. We usually know when someone is not being properly spoken about, among friends and family, or when the language and terms being used about *them* would be dishonoring to them and to God. We don't need to be rude to our palace family and friends when we speak up, but we must call others up, especially those who respect us, to the higher ground of reflecting the love of God.

Chapter 4

Jesus Came to the Table | Accept Invitations from Other Ethnic Groups

4 o'clock

> *"When they came out to see him, they begged him to stay in their village. So he stayed for two days, long enough for many more to hear his message and believe." John 4:40-41*

The Table - The Apostle Peter sat to eat with the new Gentile believers at Antioch. He enjoyed the company of these new, non-Jewish believers as they experienced their multiethnic, multi-class Christian community. But when some Jews came from Jerusalem Peter suddenly realized how his Jewish peers might judge him if they saw him sitting with the Gentiles. So, he removed himself from the table with the Gentile believers as did the other Jewish believers who were with him.

When the Apostle Paul saw what Peter had done, he openly rebuked him in front of everyone for playing the hypocrite. How did Peter, the leader of the early church, so easily stumble in representing Christ? What kind of pressure was he feeling from these other Jews? Why was sitting at a dinner table with the Gentiles such a big deal?

Jesus accepted invitations from "them"

Several times, we find Jesus entering homes and sitting at tables with groups of people that the religious leaders didn't think he should. Not only did Jesus go through Samaritan villages, but he even accepted an invitation into their homes to stay with them.

There's something powerful about inviting someone to our dinner table. There's something telling about who we invite to our tables and who we don't invite and whose homes we enter and who enters our homes. When we invite someone to our table, we are saying, "I welcome you. I want to serve you. I want to know more about you. I want to sit with you as an equal. I want to hear your story and perhaps I will have the opportunity to share my story with you."

Jesus challenges us on how we use our dinner tables, especially in relationship to those who have less than us and are in harder situations than we are. Like in Luke 14:12, Jesus turned to the host and said, "When you put on a lunch or a banquet, don't invite your friends, brothers, relatives, and rich neighbors." (I call these friends, brothers, relatives and rich neighbors, your palace community.) Instead, in Luke 14:13, Jesus tells us to invite the poor, the crippled, the lame, and the blind. At the resurrection of the righteous, God promises to reward us for inviting those who could not repay us. The table is powerful, and Jesus expects us to use our tables to further his message of love toward all. Once again, we are challenged to look outside of our comfortable circle of relationships as a starting place for showing how the love of God is greater than what the world offers.

Some people struggle with the race conversation. But in many ways, the race conversation strongly overlaps with the wealth conversation. If you build relationships across wealth gaps, you will often find it to be the same bridge needed for racial gaps. The story of "us and them" is usually tied directly to the story of "the haves and the have nots". If we look at the heart of how Jesus calls us to use our tables to love and welcome others, we will find another solution to racial and ethnic divides – the table. I call it the table, the bridge between hearts.

The Word of God clearly calls us to love those who have less or are disadvantaged. It helps us be around more of them. When we practice opening our homes and our tables like Luke 14:12-13 says, we will often find ourselves engaging with other ethnic groups.

In Matthew 25, Jesus also reminds us to not ignore the poor, the hungry, the thirsty, the prisoner, the sick, and the stranger. Jesus tells us to care for and visit those in hard situations. He said, "When you did it to one of the least of these my brothers and sisters, you were doing it to me!" (Matthew 25:40). There is a reward from Jesus when we go outside of our palace comfort to love others.

Who is at your dinner table?

First Peter 4:9 says to "cheerfully share your home with those who need a meal or a place to stay." One of the most telling measures of how far we've come in breaking down walls is who we see at our dinner tables. It is natural to invite those from our palace communities to our homes to share a meal. The challenge is to make sure we aren't only opening our homes to the us-es. The table is an opportunity to tear down walls. Communities that carry principles of division will typically show eating together, sitting at the table together, or in some cases drinking from the same fountain as off-limits. It is hard to share meals together, hear one another's stories, and continue to carry animosity.

Opening the table to others is our opportunity to learn. We've heard our palace's version of who this group is all of our lives, but how would they tell their own story? When we share our own stories, we emphasize our contributions, sacrifices and challenges, while intentionally or unintentionally sharing a little (or a lot) less about the role and impact of others. That is why it is good to have people share their own stories. That is also why we have four gospels for four different perspectives speaking to different audiences about the life of Jesus. We can benefit from them all. Our dinner conversation is an opportunity to learn about them from them. A lot of our hostility and animosity comes from what we've heard about other groups, which we then attribute to everyone in that group. Until we find ourselves in spaces and at tables where we can have meaningful interaction, our fears, prejudices, and assumptions control how we feel about others and how welcoming we are toward one another.

The Bible challenges us to be quick to listen, slow to speak, and slow to anger (James 1:19). Coming to the table is an opportunity to be quick to listen. It's possible we will get to the table and the other person may not ask us our story. That's okay. Jesus doesn't ask us to spend our time being disappointed about how they treat us, how they respond to us, or how much they want to hear our stories too.

The table is an opportunity for us to hear their stories. We want to be quick to listen. We don't want to be quick to be opinionated about or disappointed in others, especially when we have not had sufficient time to build relationships with them.

Proverbs 21:11 says that the wise man learns by listening to instruction. We love to share our stories and want others to understand our contributions, challenges, and sacrifices. We find it difficult to build healthy bridges between communities, ethnic groups, and wealth classes when we believe our contributions, challenges, and sacrifices are being belittled, overlooked, or despised. But when Jesus met the woman at the well, their conversation was rich on so many levels. Jesus listened to her and engaged so well that they were able to discuss her core religious beliefs, her greatest personal challenges, and her desire for better things.

It's no surprise there are so many negative attitudes between uses and thems. How many spaces do we really have where we can have mutually beneficial conversations? It may look like people share similar spaces, sit in the same classrooms, attend the same events. But how many times do we sit down at tables together and share our stories?

Use your dinner table to bridge divides

Jesus challenges us to use our tables to reach outside our palace relationships. Luke 14 says not to invite your friends, brothers, relatives, and rich neighbors. Jesus calls us to reach as far outside our palace communities as we can. He doesn't say for us to change our beliefs toward God. He doesn't say for us to compromise our convictions. He simply encourages us to create spaces where we can sit at tables with those who are not like us and who don't come from our worlds.

How can we really love others from a distance? How can we love others when they are on the other side of our palace walls? How can we test the truth of the stories we've heard in our palaces without hearing stories about them from them?

Hospitality is a biblical principle. It's one of the great ways we show the love of God to others. If you want to make a difference like Jesus did, invite to your table someone from another ethnic group or skin color. And don't just do it once, make it a lifestyle.

It's easy to point fingers at leaders of businesses, churches, and government and challenge their responses to the race conversation. But we will only give an account for the things that we influence and control. And we definitely control who sits at our dinner tables. We control who we invite into our living rooms to have a conversation over coffee or tea.

Maybe you've challenged your church leaders about why you don't have more ethnic groups in your church. But if we, the individuals and families, want more ethnic groups in our gatherings, let's start by having more of them at our dinner tables. A healthy relationship with them in the home is a great first step to healthy relationships in the gatherings of believers.

Those who follow Jesus learn to not focus on what to complain about but to discover how they can make a difference. God can use one person, one family, one group of friends, one church community, or maybe even the Church of the city to transform attitudes. The Bible says in Matthew 13:33 that the Kingdom of Heaven is like yeast, and the yeast causes the dough to rise. So, let's set an example of crossing cultural lines and going outside our palace communities to invite those of a different ethnic group and wealth class into our homes and to our tables.

We must have spaces for meaningful interaction with those who are not like us if anything is ever to change. When we have spent time with people who do not look like us, we learn what they are really like, not just what the media or other people say they are like. Jesus called us to be a community that knows our neighbors by name and invites our neighbors to our dinner and decision-making tables.

Chapter 5

Jesus Knew Their Story | Know Their Story

5 o'clock

> *"Jesus replied, 'Believe me, dear woman, the time is coming when it will no longer matter whether you worship the Father on this mountain or in Jerusalem. You Samaritans know very little about the one you worship, while we Jews know all about him, for salvation comes through the Jews.'" John 4:21-22*

Their story from them - For decades the story of the 1921 Tulsa Race Massacre was kept out of the history books. The Greenwood District was once a thriving community of blacks where the dollar exchanged hands some 18 times. It was burned to the ground by a mob of angry whites. The surviving black community in Tulsa, Oklahoma knew that there would be more trouble if they dared to talk about the incident in the year's following this horrifying event. Generations of Americans had no knowledge of the story of the Greenwood District that was home to Black Wall Street, which had the highest number of black millionaires in the country.

For years, minorities were told to "know their place." The knowledge that a thriving black community once existed was little known, even among blacks. The prevailing negative beliefs about the ability of blacks to thrive seemed to lack an example or a city that anyone could use as an example of Black success. Where was the proof that blacks could thrive? Where were the American cities that showed "them" in anything more than poverty and ghettoes? It would be the 21st century before the story became a part of history taught in Oklahoma schools. The history we hear often depends on who is telling the story.

Jesus acknowledged the cultural conflict

The Samaritan woman asked Jesus about who was right concerning worshipping at the mountain in Samaria versus the temple where the Jews said they should. She said, "You Jews say." When Jesus responded, he said "dear woman" and "you Samaritans" say this. Jesus understood the religious conflict behind the division. He did not ignore the history of the conflict between Samaritans and Jews. He had taken the time to learn their story.

Jesus told the woman at the well that God was not focused on either mountain. He said the time was coming "and now is" (John 4:23) that the priority would be on worship in spirit and in truth, not the place of worship. One of the core reasons behind the division between Jews and Samaritans would soon be irrelevant. Both Samaritans and Jews would be called to this simple solution to worship. She was willing to listen to what Jesus was saying because he had already demonstrated respect for her by not treating her as Jews normally would.

Jesus knew that the greater solution to ethnic division was through himself. Skin color, wealth class, blood lines, ethnic group, these core points of division would neither hinder nor help them have a better standing with God. Jesus was introducing his greater plan, that we all might be one through him.

Jesus had no problem facing the historic truths behind the ethnic division between Samaritans and Jews. How much do you know the story and history of those outside of your palace world? How much do you understand about why they respond the way they do? Knowing the story of those we are called to serve makes us more effective at loving others.

Jesus also had no problem openly talking about the fact that the Samaritans didn't know much about how to worship and who they worshipped. This may sound a bit offensive, but Jesus doesn't show favoritism. He is full of grace and tells the truth. He knew that the Samaritans had wrongly handled the worship that was passed down through Moses and he had no problem saying it. He also said that God had used the Jews in a distinct way to bring salvation to all.

Walking as one can never happen without truth, regardless of whether it puts us on a platform or brings us correction. If acknowledging the truth is personal and we find a way to reject it, we may find ourselves behaving like the Pharisees who refused the voice of John the baptizer. Humility is good for us all. We should know where our bloodlines and our ethnic groups have fallen short of the glory of God and make no excuses for it. This is where we invite Jesus to give us new hearts and to teach us to trust in Him.

Jesus was clear about what was lacking in the Samaritans understanding of God, but he did not let that stop him from telling stories of moments when they showed greater character than Jews, as in the story of the good Samaritan and story of the ten lepers who were healed and only one (the Samaritan) returned to give thanks. The palace mind is usually proud and believes we know their story and what their problem is, but their tone and the way they carry these "truths" seem to only further division. What Jesus understood about the Samaritans drew him towards them. What Jesus knew about their failure to honor the law of Moses didn't blind him from celebrating the times when they did honor the law of Moses, even better than the Jews did.

Jesus was able to see the strengths and failures of both Jews and Samaritans without drifting from his assignment or losing love toward his own palace community or those being despised. Jesus didn't come to choose sides. He came to demonstrate the kingdom of God. Jesus, full of grace and truth, was the perfect example of speaking the truth in love. Jesus showed love and understanding by knowing the history of the woman at the well's people group. He also showed that we shouldn't be afraid to talk about truths, even about ethnic groups in conflict, in a healthy and objective way.

Every ethnic group has strengths and weaknesses. We stay blind when we fail to see our own faults and overemphasize our strengths.

We equally fail when we consistently focus on the faults of others and can find little to no good in them.

We know that even though all ethnic groups have strengths and weaknesses, ultimately all have sinned and fall short of the glory of God (Romans 3:23). Jesus came to lay down his life as the lamb slain from the foundation of the world to take away the sins of the world (John 1:29). In him, we move beyond ethnic division and misunderstanding. We are called to let our lights shine and boldly show a love that is greater, so the world can clearly see who Jesus is.

Speak with grace and truth

"Jesus replied, 'Believe me, dear woman, the time is coming when it will no longer matter whether you worship the Father on this mountain or in Jerusalem'" (John 4:21). When Jesus says, "Dear woman," he isn't speaking in a condescending way, but rather tenderly speaking to her with grace and truth.

Not only was he breaking social laws by speaking to a Samaritan in the first place, but he is also speaking tenderly with care. I wonder whether the woman ever imagined a Jewish man speaking to her in such a way. Who from outside your palace community have you shocked with your genuine concern and affection?

Often us-es and thems have a hard time speaking to and hearing each other. We can be quick to take offense and quick to point out "truth" with very little "grace." To reach the oneness that Jesus prayed for, we must follow his example. If we want to understand the stories of other ethnic groups and keep those stories subject to the ultimate plan of the Father, the level of "truth" we claim to have must be mixed with at least an equal amount of grace.

The Apostle Paul recognized the power and value of his ethnic group when he boasted of being a Hebrew of Hebrews circumcised on the eighth day of the tribe of Benjamin. He was a Pharisee of Pharisees, so he makes the greatest boast possible, that in the flesh no one could compare with him when it came to being able to boast of his ethnic group. But he only used his ethnicity to further the truth of the love of God, the cross of Christ, and the power of the Gospel. He didn't use it as an excuse to treat others as untouchables or avoid being in spaces where Gentiles were.

The challenge to learn about other ethnic groups leads us to a place of need (1 Corinthians 12:15-26). Rather than only hearing the stories that make us look good and appear as the heroes, we seek to learn a fuller history that includes the stories of other ethnic groups, regardless of whether our contribution was good, bad or both. Rather than relying on our palace education about other groups, we seek to learn about their sacrifices, challenges, and contributions from them.

If we want to be more like Jesus, we begin by acknowledging our need to rise above human nature, which is to no longer make ourselves the center of the world. Learning to focus on others and appreciate them opens a whole new world. In fact, we may discover that it's easier to build relationships with those outside our palace when we are making a genuine effort to appreciate who they are. Therefore, we seek guides (books, leaders, teachers, museums, and other resources) from within their community to help us learn. Learning about others is a way to show that you value them.

Find a person of peace

There is a principle in the Scriptures that Jesus taught the disciples. When they were sent to different cities and countries, they were to find a house with a person of peace where they could stay. Missionaries to other countries understand this. When they find a person native to the country, they can learn where to go and how to communicate. They can learn customs and values, what not to be offended by, and how not to offend. There is greater success in relating to those we are seeking to love when we have the help of a guide, or a person of peace.

Finding that person of peace is wisdom. Proverbs 24:6 says, "Don't go to war without wise guidance. There is safety in many counselors."

When we carry a humility toward others, we are open to learning more about them from them. We start to move away from thoughts like, "If only they would do this, this would change" or "If they were more like us, they would succeed." These thoughts often come from those who don't understand the challenges other communities face.

While it is true there are clear paths to change for anyone, it's also harder to reach a group of people without knowing their story and recognizing their challenges and the level of sacrifice needed to prosper in their world. If we don't know their contributions and what they're already doing, it will be harder to meet them with grace and truth.

Seek to understand their story

Fences can separate us and make it hard to communicate with one another. Offenses can do the same thing. So we want to avoid terms, inferences, or behaviors that are offensive to someone else's culture and community. We want to be mindful of the words we choose. We show value for others by taking the time to learn how to communicate well.

We want to learn about others' cultures so their communication, responses, and reactions toward us don't cause us to take things personally, respond according to our inherited palace behaviors, or simply begin to withdraw and close our hearts. We want to respond like Jesus responds. Jesus did not get offended when the woman at the well said "you Jews" or when she asked challenging and direct questions. He was prepared to create a bridge of hope so she could understand and know that he was the Messiah. This is what we want too! We want our conversation and our responses to draw people to Jesus not push them away.

If our offense, or our palace community's offense, becomes more important than us giving others the opportunity to hear the beautiful story of how "God so loved the world that he gave his only begotten son" (John 3:16), then our offense has blinded us, and we are no longer representing Jesus and his plans. Jesus stayed ready to share the full story of the Father's plan. He told the Samaritan woman that the future he was preparing was not just for the Jews but for all who would worship him in spirit and in truth. We too should prepare to not offend others and to not be quick to take offense.

Chapter 6

Jesus Was a Blessing to Them | Be a Blessing to Them

6 o'clock

"Jesus replied, 'If you only knew the gift God has for you and who you are speaking to, you would ask me, and I would give you living water.'" John 4:10

Know their names – "Good morning, Hassan!" The hotel rep paused and stared as the African American consultant, who had just greeted him, walked past. "Good morning, sir," Hassan replied. Noticing that Hassan wanted to say something, the consultant paused. (The two had met the day before at check-in. The consultant had taken a few extra minutes to learn Hassan's name and a little bit of his story—making sure he pronounced his name correctly.)

Hassan took a deep breath, paused from his work and said, "I've worked here for three years and that is the first time any guest has called me by my name."

Jesus sought the good of those outside his palace

In order to develop relationships, we must close the distance between us and them. We could wait for them to come to us or we could do what Jesus did to love the Samaritans. We could go to them. Jesus travelled outside of his palace community and purposefully went to them.

Jesus tells us to go into the world and teach all nations (*ethnos*). We have been given an assignment to go into all the world and make disciples of all ethnic groups. This means we are called to live lives that are not ethnically homogeneous. We do this by finding ways to be around those of different ethnic groups and wealth classes. God's solution to the distance between us and them is for us to take responsibility for closing the gap and go. Be a part of loving people outside of your own world.

In Luke 4:18-19 Jesus says, "The Spirit of the Lord is upon me, for he has anointed me to bring Good News to the poor." It's the responsibility of those with resources and mobility to go share the Good News and show the love of God to those who are in need. We shouldn't expect them to come to our palaces to seek us out.

Matthew 5:14-16 says that our light shines when we do good works. Find ways to serve and participate in loving those who are in need and are outside of your palace community of relationships. Help them flourish and beautify their lives, their families, and their communities. "No one lights a lamp and then puts it under a basket. (Matthew 5:15a)" Don't just do good works to your palace friends who will pay you back. Go serve and love people in places where your good deeds will shine "so that everyone will praise your heavenly Father. (Matthew 5:16)"

Our best path towards being present in the community of others and being welcomed in their spaces is by serving side-by-side. Serving together, lifting others, and sacrificing your time and resources "them" is how we build trust and tear down walls of division. Doors open when your love for others is backed with action. Hearts open when your presence is not just a quick volunteer opportunity, but a sacrificial commitment to partner and care through successes and challenges.

The idea of worshipping side-by-side will be a natural overflow after we start inviting them to our tables, learning more about them, and showing up to be a part of solutions in their communities.

Serving is central to loving others well. I'm sure you've heard the quote that says, "People don't care how much you know until they know how much you care." Well said! Doing good works and letting our lights shine before others is how we drive out the darkness of hatred and bitterness.

Matthew 25:35 calls us to care for those who are suffering. Whether that's caring for those without clothes, drink, or places to stay or those in prison or considered immigrants and refugees, we are called to care for strangers. This is not political. This is a question for how we are using our own time and resources. It's calling us to care in the ways that Jesus called us to care and to help those who are suffering.

Our obedience to this call automatically puts us in spaces around other ethnic groups and wealth classes. Ministering to those who are suffering opens the door for us to serve a population that is multi-ethnic and multi-class. Jesus said that when we do these works it is the same as us doing them to him (Matthew 25:31-46):

- Feeding the hungry and thirsty
- Showing hospitality
- Providing clothing
- Visiting the sick
- Visiting those in prison

Are you a worshipper? Do you want to love Jesus? In Matthew 25:40, we find a beautiful way to love Him that doesn't require singing or musical talent. Jesus tells us what he will say to those that will be welcomed into his kingdom after this life. He will say, when you served "the least of these my brothers and sisters, you were doing it to me!" James adds that pure religion (James 1:27) is caring for orphans and widows. James connects pure religion to how we show up for those whose families have faced crises. If we do the good works that Jesus called us to do, we will have opportunity to engage outside our palace community. We can almost be sure that we will be around other ethnic groups and most definitely other wealth classes.

So, how do we find spaces where we can be around them? Look for the poor, the rundown neighborhoods, the struggling schools, the prisons, the hospitals, the nursing homes, the empty playgrounds, and the streets. Look outside of your palace world. Love like Jesus loved, seek those who Jesus sought, and go where Jesus went.

I remember going to a foreign country that was a 12-hour time difference from Oklahoma. We spent weeks learning how to not be offensive, how to communicate, and how to be relatable when sharing our stories about how Jesus had changed our lives.

One of our first trips was to a prison yard filled with young men. They gathered to us at the little chapel in the middle of the prison yard to see why these foreigners had come. I was trying to remember all the rules we had learned until our translator clearly told us that those rules don't apply inside the prison yard.

All the rules of caution about saying the name of Jesus were no longer valid. The guards didn't care what we told the prisoners. In their society, these young men were now considered the scum of the earth, worthless. If we were worried about us and our stories of Jesus being received by their ethnic group, we had to worry no longer. They received us.

Many of the young men who were scowling at us were weeping with hope less than an hour later. God had sent someone from the palace country of America to love them, the forgotten of their own community, and share the Good News.

Are you wondering whether or not you will be received by "them" (that other ethnic group)? One easy place to start is to go where you are needed, invited, and welcomed. Go beyond your palace walls to humbly serve those in need. Be a mentor. Visit those who are sick and suffering. Find solutions for under-resourced communities.

Show up to be a blessing where the needs are the greatest. Jesus went to those whom his palace community rejected and looked down on—the poor, the lepers, and the Samaritans.

When we live like Jesus, love like Jesus, and pursue those who Jesus pursued, we will automatically begin to tear down social and cultural walls of division. We will have more empathy when we speak to them and about them. We will have compassion like Jesus did towards our need.

Jesus redefines what it means to be Samaritan

It is not hard to discover how Jesus solves the "race problem." The answer is hidden in plain sight, and it is brilliant. We can learn Jesus's attitude toward other ethnic groups by looking at every mention of the terms "Samaria" and "Samaritan" in the Bible. When we do this, we find two stories that help us understand how intentional Jesus was in embracing other ethnic groups: the Good Samaritan and the Samaritan leper who Jesus healed.

In the story of the Good Samaritan (Luke 10:29-37), Jesus throws his palace community under the bus and definitely doesn't make them the heroes of the story. He exposes the two respected leaders of the Jewish community—the priest and the Levite—and shares a story of the Levite and priest walking past a man beaten and left half dead.

Perhaps the Levite and the Priest had no care for the man who was suffering because they only sought to do good deeds when others were watching. Maybe they were scared that the thieves or other evil people were nearby. Either way, they walked right by, and Jesus identified this as a lack of compassion and failure to "love your neighbor as yourself."

But a Samaritan stopped to care for the person in need. Jesus highlighted a Samaritan, one considered lowly and unclean in the eyes of Jews, showing greater virtue than the religious leaders of the Jewish community. The Samaritan changed his schedule and used his own money to make sure the injured man was able to get on his feet again. Of all the stories Jesus could tell to explain loving your neighbor, he chose the one where the Samaritan was the hero of the story.

Another story where Jesus mentions a Samaritan distinctly is in Luke 17:11-19, where ten lepers were healed, but only one returned to give thanks. Jesus makes sure we know that this one person was a Samaritan.

Here are two stories, the Good Samaritan who helped a stranger and the Samaritan leper who got healed. Jesus brilliantly deconstructed their wrong attitudes toward others by speaking positively about Samaritans. In doing so, he put Jews in a position to learn from their stories.

Do you learn from the strengths and virtues of other ethnic groups? Or do you only listen to your palace community and those who have more power, wealth, and influence than you? What if a greater understanding of God and his ways is waiting for you to discover through the example of those who are considered Samaritans to your palace community? What if those you despise are modeling the character of Jesus in a way that your offenses won't allow you to appreciate?

Jesus tells the story of the Good Samaritan as a model of the Second Greatest Commandment by highlighting and making a positive example of someone the Jews' palace community was never encouraged to learn from. He understood that the Samaritans were despised, and this only strengthened his point by telling the Jews, who felt holier than the Samaritans, that it was a Samaritan who loved his neighbor well.

Jesus saw the one leper out of the ten that got healed returning, and he was a Samaritan. So he says, "Was no one found to return and give praise to God except this foreigner?" Once again, Jesus was not afraid to talk about other ethnic groups.

Notice that Jesus used his voice and platform to show Samaritans demonstrating model character. This made opportunity for mutual respect to grow. Normally, when Jews mentioned a Samaritan, it was to give another reason to despise them and maintain their division. Jesus did not mention the man's Samaritan ethnicity in a condescending way. Both the story of the Good Samaritan and the Samaritan leper who was healed showed Samaritans in a positive light.

Highlight what is good about "them"

We often look for pictures and stories where we show the community we're serving in their need, but Jesus chose to show the positive and strong characteristics of a community that was despised. Jesus knows our palace pride, our palace postures, and how we take ethnic positions of superiority over others.

He knows that even if we don't have more money than the other ethnic group or more land and wealth, we will claim we have more integrity, righteousness, and character than them and that they are the ones who are bad and greedy. We love to share our stories to put ourselves in a positive light. We tell stories so the us-es look good and the thems look bad. This is standard human behavior.

That's the problem. So Jesus flips it. He knows the Jews like to see themselves in a positive light. So he chooses to put the Samaritans in a positive light, whether they are on the receiving end of grace and healing as with the Samaritan or with the ten lepers being healed and only the Samaritan returning.

In the story of the Good Samaritan, the Samaritan is in the giving position not the receiving. Often, when it comes to serving others, the images we see are just how poor and needy the other ethnic groups are and how strong, giving, and self-sufficient our group is, implying that they desperately need us. Jesus mentions that they were a Samaritan so he may improve the way the Samaritans are looked upon. He chooses to celebrate great character coming from a Samaritan and share their strengths.

This is so important when it comes to entering another community by serving. Often, we feel so great about ourselves because we have left our palaces and are "sacrificing" to be there for others. We see our dignity, our righteousness, our sacrificial behavior as a badge to wear on our sleeves. But Jesus mentioned other ethnic groups in that positive light and laid the foundation for mutual respect.

Seek good for others

Proverbs 21:13 says, "Those who shut their ears to the cries of the poor will be ignored in their own time of need." We are clearly called to help those in need. We can find lots of common ground among those who love Jesus and with others in our cities when we simply seek to care for one another in the areas of suffering, disease, affliction, loss, and pain.

Proverbs 22:16 says, "A person who gets ahead by oppressing the poor or by showering gifts on the rich will end in poverty." The wisdom of Solomon tells us that oppressing "them" and showering gifts on our rich friends is not wisdom and it is not his way. There are a thousand ways to get rich off of the poor, but the righteous don't seek to take advantage of others. We are called to lift those who are down, and we are not to show special favor towards the rich for personal advantage. The rich are inundated with people who have their own motives and who want to be in their favor. Seek favor with God and he will touch the hearts of those who are called to favor you. Love those that God says to love and watch him open the doors of peoples' hearts.

Proverbs 11:27 says, "If you search for good, you will find favor; but if you search for evil, it will find you!" If we want to be great bridge builders and ministers of reconciliation, this scripture tells us to seek their good. This is following the example of Jesus. Acts 10:38 says, "Jesus went around doing good." Do you really want to heal divides? Do good. Go into their communities, serve their vision without having to lead everything and simply do good. Build trust by investing good deeds into the people and the communities that have experienced animosity or pain from your palace community.

We may be able to change laws to force "us and them" to behave well towards one another, but there is nothing like relationships being healed from the heart. This is called favor. We want to grow in favor. Jesus told the story of the good Samaritan so generations would admire his good deed and we have. His good deeds has birthed favor in our hearts towards the term Samaritan.

Luke 2:52 says that Jesus grew in favor with God and man, and we want to grow in favor with those who are outside of our ethnic group. If we want to turn away from palace conversations, murmuring and complaining, and talking down about other groups, then we can begin to grow in favor with other ethnic groups by serving them and working side-by-side to help address the human suffering in their communities.

Serving in places where nothing but love is the reason you show up is a simple way to grow in favor and build bridges. As long as we stay in our palaces and tell others to pull themselves up by their bootstraps, we are missing an opportunity to see the fulfillment of Jesus's prayer in John 17:21. We will seldom be pushed away when we sincerely show up, not to tell people how to do things, but to solve problems together, to first value and appreciate the leadership, their determination, their sacrifice and the price that they are already paying to make a difference in their communities. It's easy for outsiders to boast of what they would do if they were in the same situation, whether that be prosperity, poverty or another skin color. That is not the way to build bridges. You will find that their hearts may open to you more quickly if you simply serve and take the time to first value and appreciate who they are and the work that they do. When Jesus showed up, he didn't start his ministry until he honored the ministry of John the Baptist. Honor is a core attribute of those who serve in God's kingdom. Dishonor and belittling the work and sacrifice of others is a foundation for prolonged division.

So, let's go into other communities like Jesus did. Let's value others. You may also do this by taking time to learn how to properly pronounce their names and not give them a new name that is easier for you to say. These are subtle paternalistic behaviors that don't give value to the community we are seeking to serve. This is what Nebuchadnezzar did to Daniel and his friends. He renamed them. He showed his authority and dominance by naming them, according to his culture, rather than regarding the names given them from their own culture.

When we reference others when they are not around, remember to be careful not to fall into the condescending tone of a negative palace conversation. When we bring up their names with respect and dignity behind closed doors, we won't find ourselves "accidentally" saying something offensive when they are around.

Acknowledging people's names is a way to show value. When someone gives us permission based on relationship to call them by another fun name, then feel free to do so, but only then. Be careful of doing like slave masters who threw away the African names of their slaves and gave them different names. Be careful of showing subtle dominance by not taking time to pronounce their name correctly.

Jesus sought to be a blessing to others and he refused to join his ethnic group in looking down on Samaritans. It's easier to remember other groups with value and respect if we take time to hear their stories and challenges. There is character among the Samaritans (those outside of our palace relationships), and there are Jews (those who have wealth and greater resources) who have grace and truth. All of "us" aren't good and all of "them" aren't bad. As Jesus said in John 7:24, "look beneath the surface so you can judge correctly." Be careful of generalizations and give people the opportunity to be known for who they are. In our palace conversations and palace communities, we're not used to hearing positive stories about them, so Jesus made sure to be in spaces where he could hear their stories and encounter who they really are. He did not allow the negative palace stories that he heard about Samaritans cause him to keep distance and reject them like his palace community of Jews did. He represented God's heart towards them and was intentional about showing that love in Samaria and outside of his familiar, Jewish world.

Chapter 7

Jesus Brought People Together | Bring People Together

7 o'clock

> *"Just then his disciples came back. They were shocked to find him talking to a woman, but none of them had the nerve to ask, 'What do you want with her?' or 'Why are you talking to her?'" John 4:27*

Bring us and them together – In January of 2015, I had the idea of inviting an ethnically mixed group of leaders to watch the new Martin Luther King Jr. movie called Selma on opening night. Seventy leaders responded to the invitation and showed up to watch the movie on the "other" side of town and to gather for food and conversation afterwards. The movie did not disappoint and neither did the conversations.

After thirty minutes of everyone taking turns sharing at their tables about personal reflections on the movie, it was time for each table to share a special story that they heard during this time, with the larger group. No one expected what would happen next.

A middle-aged woman introduced herself as the granddaughter of an offender in the Tulsa Race Massacre. She spoke of how her family was on the wrong side of history and she asked forgiveness for their wrongs. No one expected her to do this, and no one expected her acknowledgement to have the impact that it did, but the sound of emotion from blacks and whites in the room could not be ignored. This opportunity for healing and acknowledgement happened because a space was made for a group of us and them to be at the table together and to address a topic that would typically stay buried, even among longtime friends who were from different ethnic groups.

Jesus built bridges between groups

Jesus made opportunities for his Jewish disciples and the Samaritans to be in the same spaces. In the story of Jesus sending his disciples to find him a place and then being rejected by the Samaritans, the Bible made sure we knew that Jesus was going through Samaria (not around it).

Going through Samaria was one more way Jesus was intentional about tearing down walls, inherited habits, and negative mentalities that hindered his disciples from loving their neighbors as themselves. Most Jews avoided going through Samaria at all costs. Jews would not have been seen interacting with or going into Samaritan communities to buy food. But Jesus intentionally sent his disciples into the Samaritan village to buy food (John 4:8).

Jesus did not live by his palace community's culture. He lived by heaven's culture and always sought to please his Father. We are called to do the same. Jesus intentionally went through Samaria for us to catch a glimpse of his desire for our different people groups to be one in Christ and to plant the seeds for the fulfillment of his prayer in John 17:21.

It takes more than brief interactions and working at the same jobs with other ethnic groups to overcome inherited beliefs, prejudices, suspicions, and fears. To reach wholeness, relationships must be built, and there must be a way to have quality time together with meaningful interaction. Jesus knew his disciples would not be changed overnight, so he made sure that at the very least his route sent his Jewish disciples into the territory of the Samaritans often. He made sure that his disciples would have the opportunity to love Samaritans in practice and not just "in their hearts".

Have you considered adjusting your life routes to include spaces that aren't so homogenous? Can you think of ways your inner circle, team, or family could be in spaces where you could authentically connect with people from different ethnic and cultural backgrounds?

Jesus intentionally went through the spaces of other ethnic groups because he wanted his disciples to increase their comfort level in non-palace interactions and relationships. The Great Commission (Matthew 28:19-20) is centered on going into all the world, so Jesus wanted to make being around those outside of their world a normal part of his disciples' lives.

When Jesus assessed the homogenous world of his disciples, he knew they needed to be in spaces where they could meet and interact with Samaritans themselves. What great preparation to fulfill the Great Commission! If they spent their whole lives in spaces where they had so few non-palace interactions or relationships, how could they love well and carry God's heart to other ethnic groups with grace and not pride?

John 4:27 notes that when the disciples returned from buying food, they "were shocked to find him talking to a woman." Interestingly, Scripture doesn't say they were shocked that he was talking to a Samaritan, but that he was talking to a woman (breaking even more social norms!). This implies that they were not shocked that Jesus was talking to a Samaritan. Perhaps they had already become accustomed to Jesus engaging Samaritans.

Every time Jesus spoke to a Samaritan, engaged Samaritans, talked with Samaritans, went through Samaria, he boldly declared that something new was present: the Kingdom of Heaven. These were glimpses of Revelation 7:9 where every nation, tribe, and tongue would be present before the throne of God.

The woman at the well invited herself to be Jesus's partner. She invited all the men in the city to come see Jesus. What a powerful partnership! It was an instant move of God. It all happened because Jesus made Samaria a part of his normal route and rejected the cultural tendency to avoid them and their communities. Why would

Jesus go outside of normal palace behavior? Because he was acting with the Father's greater plan in mind. He wasn't just living according to what was familiar and comfortable.

Build bridges as a lifestyle

The social walls that have been built in our world through offense and hurt are what we as the body of Christ can tear down. By consistently finding opportunity to be around "them," or by having our family, staff, or organization include their spaces and gathering spots as places we frequent, we can do what Jesus did. We are making opportunity to meet others who may also want to be a part of seeing God's will fulfilled with us.

To learn to love those outside our palace takes time. Healing generational divides is not an easy one-time-fix, but Jesus does make the path clear and practical. Find the spaces where the thems live, eat, hang out, celebrate, and participate. Then think of ways to invite them to activities or events where your palace community will be present.

Relationships have doors. It's much easier to gain someone's trust when we have gotten to know them personally. To bridge gaps will take intentional introductions. It will take someone purposefully seeking to get both parties in the same space where they can interact.

There are people who could work dynamically together and potentially change the world, but they may never meet because their worlds are too far apart. Think about those in your palace community. How many of them will ever be in situations where they could hear the stories you've heard or meet the people you've met? This is why we also must be bridge builders and connectors. Think of opportunities to introduce your non-palace friends to those in your palace communities.

At this point in the journey, we may be growing in love and relationship with "them," but we may also be intentionally or unintentionally keeping our worlds separate. Some people are not interested in discovering how their palace friends will respond to their new non-palace community. They aren't ready to be seen breaking the social law of getting too comfortable with them. So, they serve "across town" with them, but they hang out and build relationship with "us." Even though they are being more engaged with non-palace friends, they intentionally keep their two worlds separate out of fear and reluctance.

After Jesus ascended and the other ethnic groups began to join the church, there was a moment where Peter did this very thing. He was enjoying eating and connecting with the Gentiles, but when his Jewish palace community showed up from Jerusalem, he distanced himself from the Gentiles. Paul called out his hypocrisy, and Peter received the rebuke because he knew he was not representing God's heart.

Jesus made opportunity for the us-them wall to crumble by bringing his palace community of disciples into the presence of Samaritans. Bridge builders don't have to make any relationships happen, but opportunities for greater things increase when a bridge is present. Be intentional about being a bridge. Do what Jesus did.

There are those in your palace world who respect your voice and your character to the point that they will follow you and hear your insights. Be intentional about introducing your palace and non-palace friends to one another. Be an active part of establishing the beautiful narrative of different ethnic groups working together in love to serve and bless others.

There are things in your daily life that will make opportunity for bringing us and them together. Invite them to your birthday party. Invite their children to your child's birthday party. Use their restaurant to cater your food. Enjoy their services and their stores. You don't have to take months to create a big event. At this level, simply include them in your life and be intentional about using opportunities to introduce them to your us-community and your us-community to them.

There is an order to the ideas presented in this book. By making each chapter a lifestyle, you open the door to the next idea. When you frequent the restaurants and hangout places of others, open your dinner table, take time to learn their stories, and begin serving side-by-side, you will experience new friendships and relationships.

Who from a different group do you know personally that you could invite? Invite them into one of your spaces, your home, or an event where you can bring different groups together. That's being a bridge builder. That's exercising the ministry of reconciliation. That's making an opportunity for us-es and thems to meet. We don't have to make anything happen. We can simply make introductions. We can bring people into spaces where they can grow in value for one another.

While I've said many things to watch out for concerning your palace, I don't want you to hate the people in your palace! If you begin to hate those in your palace, all we have succeeded in doing is creating another us-them scenario, where now the us-es are those spending time outside of homogeneous spaces and the thems are those who are still in homogeneous spaces.

It's possible to get to tomorrow without having to label someone as the bad guy. It's possible to behave and think like Jesus, who shared openly wherever he went that the Kingdom of Heaven was present.

So, this is not just a hope for an unreachable and distant future. Jesus prayed in John 17:21 that we would be one right now. That's *before* we all pass into eternity.

The beauty of Christian community

I am an African American male. If someone sees me sitting at a table with all African American males, it is no shock to them that I would find some level of camaraderie, engagement, or common ground with this group. However, when we are found sitting at tables, having authentic conversations, and building community between ethnic groups that have known animosity, then our actions start shouting a message of hope that is hard to ignore.

Perhaps we would have to make fewer public statements about where we stand on the topic of race, if it were normal for different ethnic groups of believers to be found serving together, worshipping together, and being in community together for the cause of Christ. No one had to ask Jesus about his thoughts on Samaritans. His actions made his position clear, not for political reasons, but simply to reflect the Father's heart.

His strategy was to operate on offense, not defense. No one had to ask whether he believed that "love your neighbor as yourself" included the Samaritans too. His values were clear. We also don't have to leave others wondering whether we have let go of offense or if we have a genuine love beyond ethnic division. If people must go looking for our light in that area, then we are lacking in being a "city set on a hill which cannot be hidden" (Matthew 5:14). Do what Jesus did and others will see more clearly how to love others too. Jesus is our example, and our obedience will produce the beauty of Christian community that crosses age groups, socioeconomic status, and ethnicity.

Those who intentionally create spaces for us-es and thems to learn one another's names, get to know one another, and move beyond the walls and issues that divide us are helping to fulfill Jesus's prayer that we would be one. As we make opportunities for our palace and non-palace friends to meet, we also have opportunity to make non-palace friends. We don't *have* to become friends, but it sure makes working together a lot easier. Jesus had a goal of friendship with his disciples (John 15:14-15), so why wouldn't we consider growing in our non-palace relationships also.

There are different levels of friendship. We open our hearts to others based on trust. I am amazed at how fast Jesus was able to win the trust of the Samaritan woman at the well. He addressed some touchy topics in their brief conversation. When she asked for the living water he offered, Jesus tells her to go and get her husband. "I don't have a husband," the woman replied. Jesus said, "You're right! You don't have a husband—for you have had five husbands, and you aren't even married to the man you're living with now. You certainly spoke the truth!" (John 4:17-18).

She sees the power of God, opens up, and acknowledges Jesus as a prophet. Within a few minutes, one of her hardest life secrets was being addressed. It was probably shameful for her to carry such a reputation in her community. This could be why she was at the well at an hour when people didn't normally go. But she didn't get combative. She opened up to Jesus.

Since Jesus supernaturally exposed her secret during this one-on-one conversation, she didn't have the chance to refuse to open up. She didn't have the opportunity to wait to get to know this Jewish man before she shared all her business. All that was left was to see how Jesus would handle this sensitive information.

Not one shaming word came from Jesus. He was not looking for something negative about her. His goal wasn't to condescend or put Samaritans "in their place." He spoke the truth, made no jokes, called her no names, and did not roll his eyes upon hearing how many marriages she had experienced Jesus treated her with dignity. He stayed fully present and continued to answer her questions and reveal himself to her. To heal ethnic divides, we must be gracious with the challenges of others. The Bible says to "rejoice with those who do rejoice" and "weep with those who weep" (Romans 12:15). When was the last time you celebrated something that was important to them? When was the last time you mourned the loss of something that was important them? Connection matters. Connection builds trust. Trust is a gift and so are relationships. As we consider who in our palace world would love to meet our non-palace friends, continue to grow in your relationships with your non-palace friends. Think of ways that your lives may intersect or that you could have fun together just like you would if they were a palace friend. The stronger our relationship are, the more we will be able to make a difference together and help one another bless our cities and communities.

If we want to make the best opportunity to have a future where we work together with mutual esteem, then be a person others can trust with the things that matter to them the most. These are their stories of pain, loss, and challenge. It will be difficult for a multiethnic society to move into a greater level of healing if there isn't a mutual respect for one another's histories.

We can't expect to have authentic relationships with others if we are not willing to respect the sacrifices, challenges, and contributions that they and their people groups have made to give us things that we all enjoy. To not value those contributions is to not value them.

Make opportunity for friendship by hearing one another's stories, respecting one another's stories, making room for one another, and learning from one another. Be a great friend, just like you would to one of your own. Reject any temptation to treat their story and their challenges as irrelevant. Jesus took a few minutes to show the Samaritan woman the Father's heart, and her life was changed.

In Philippians 3:10, Paul said this about knowing Jesus, "That I may know him and the power of his resurrection and the fellowship of his sufferings." There's something about respecting one another's sufferings that affects whether the relationship goes any further. If we want to be trusted and build relationships that are going to help us become the John 17:21 community that Jesus prayed for, it requires investing the time to hear and understand where someone else is coming from.

Palace walls are strong. We all have friends and relatives who respect us and who may never meet people outside of their palace unless we lead them there. Let's be intentional about building stronger relationships with those outside of our palace community and bringing people from different groups together.

Chapter 8

Jesus Sent Teams | Work Together to Be More Effective

8 o'clock

"The woman left her water jar beside the well and ran back to the village, telling everyone, 'Come and see a man who told me everything I ever did! Could he possibly be the Messiah?' So the people came streaming from the village to see him." John 4:28-30

We are stronger together – Having lost his public office in a heated political battle, Wes now wondered how God would use him. It was time to seek God about how to use his life and influence for the glory of God. He started to wonder what would happen if his peers, other Christian leaders, who were well-known and kind, decided to start working together with an intentional plan to bless their cities. Now over a decade later his leadership training has made an impact across Oklahoma.

Wes and I sat across the table at Charleston's as I listened to his amazing plan. This was our first time connecting after we met as perfect strangers standing in a line at a dinner just days earlier. As the years passed, we came to realize that we both had a burning shared vision to see God bless our city. Our brief and sporadic conversations seemed to fuel both of us as we both went after big and crazy dreams to see God's grace reach the challenges in our city or in his words, "Discover what our Daddy (speaking of God) is willing to do."

It soon became obvious to both of us that, though we came from different worlds, any time we spent together made both of us more effective and kept us both more encouraged in the journey towards God's dreams for the city. We finally decided to join together as prayer partners, committing to meet for prayer, vision, and connection weekly. We prayed. We talked. We challenged one another's beliefs and responses, especially around race and the topic of unity in the body of Christ.

Our commitment to prayer and time spent gave us the trust we needed to discuss pretty much any heavy topic without filtering our words. Our time together made us both better in relating to those outside of our palace communities. We empowered one another to be better at blessing a multi-ethnic city. Healthy multi-ethnic partnerships can move us from the pain in the streets to wholeness at the table of friendship.

Jesus declared a new "us"

There is a story in Matthew 12, where Jesus was teaching a group of followers. Jesus's mother and siblings—his natural family—were outside seeking to speak with him. You know how family can be, no matter who you are or what you're doing. Family members generally believe we have special rights and privileges with one another. In this situation, Jesus's family was literally wanting to interrupt his meeting and speak to him.

When they crossed this line and sought family preference, Jesus had to make some things clear. He said, "Anyone who does the will of my Father in heaven is my brother and sister and mother!" (Matthew 12:50). This is a powerful statement on several levels. Jesus declares who his true "us" group really is. He is giving this right to a group that could include or exclude his blood relatives. This is the secret as to why Jewish culture and their behavior toward Samaritans never molded his life. He would only be molded and influenced by the behaviors of those who walked with and trusted God.

We don't get to choose our bloodlines and ethnic groups, but we do get to choose the "family" with whom we identify in values and vision. For Jesus, his family is the family of "doers" as James will call them in James 1:22-25. These are the people who do the will of his Father. He said that the people who were his real family were not so much his flesh and blood as those who were putting his teachings to practice.

Jesus declared a new us, a bold statement. He wanted to be identified in a family picture with those who do the will of his Father over a family picture with those who had the same nose shape, skin color, eye color, bloodline, etc.

Jesus declared that God's family is based on our character and choices. In one of the longest recorded back-and-forth arguments between Jesus and the Jews of his palace community, Jesus contends there is a difference between claiming to be in God's family and truly living with God as Father (John 8:31-59). He said the children of Abraham are those who do the works of Abraham more so than those of his flesh and blood.

When we declare a new us, there is less need to be taught how to love others. We naturally care for and defend those we consider our own. We see the things that affect them as affecting us, so we have a personal interest in and a high commitment to their success. So, who do we consider one of "us"?

Working together

As far as Jesus is concerned, "us" includes anyone from any ethnic group or wealth class who does the Father's will. It is our responsibility to make sure those we consider us include those Jesus considers us.

If our us fails to include those from among the thems who do God's will, then our churches, movements, organizations, and businesses in the body of Christ will be more of a reflection of our palace communities than a manifestation of what heaven will look like. Our path to seeing ethnic groups serve and worship together has everything to do with our individual willingness to be intentional toward the thems, like Jesus was.

When the Samaritan woman received Jesus's message, she went through the streets, told her story, invited her countrymen and pointed the way. Jesus didn't have to do anything but wait for half of the city to come to him. What a beautiful picture of an us cooperating with someone considered a them to his palace community. This was a Jew and a Samaritan working together to further God's plans.

Who could you team up with outside of your palace for the glory of God? Where do you have opportunity for such a relationship to become a reality?

Jesus shows up in the Samaritan's space. This is how he makes opportunity for connection. The Bible says that "the people came streaming from the village to see him" (John 4:30). It goes on to say, "Many Samaritans from the village believed in Jesus" and "they begged him to stay in their village. So, he stayed for two days, long enough for many more to hear his message and believe" (John 4:39-42). Throw away the fear and reluctance of being around them. Do what Jesus did.

This all came from one brief encounter between an us and a them. Jesus found a partner in an unlikely vessel—someone who was the wrong ethnic group, wrong gender, and wrong kind of reputation. May we not overlook those outside of our ethnic groups and wealth classes who God want us to receive.

I am looking forward to seeing more partnerships and teams working together across ethnic and wealth divides to help the church live out Jesus's prayer for our oneness and to fulfill the Great Commission together. These dynamic teams will more effectively reach the world and our ethnically diverse communities.

Don't wait in your palace expecting a multiethnic team to come to you. Go where Jesus went. This can be as simple as going across town and serving another community.

If we learn to love well in our cities, we will be ready to do the same when we are called to go to another country. This is the opportunity Jesus gave his disciples because of his brilliant and intentional leadership. Talking to Samaritans was familiar to the disciples because Jesus led them into spaces where they would meet Samaritans.

Are you leading your family, your organization, or your friend group deeper into your comfortable palace of us-es or out into the fields around thems?

One family, one mission

Why is family important? Because Jesus uses this picture in Matthew 12:48 to help us understand his invitation to us. Family may be a sore spot for some people, but we must not lose vision for restoring families and talking about what a healthy family looks like. One of the secrets of prayer is to not let pain redefine what is God's best for us all. The term family is important to understand because that's what Jesus considers us. If he considers us family, then we must see one another as family.

A healthy family works together to see each person's success. This doesn't throw out accountability, but being family does mean we are willing to sacrifice to see one another succeed. We see this in Numbers 32 when Moses reprimands two tribes of Israel that had already settled in the promised land for being slow to come to the aid of their fellow Israelites who still needed to fight foes to occupy their lands. Moses said to them, "Do you intend to stay here while your brothers go across and do all the fighting?" (Numbers 32:6).

What if the body of Christ walked in love and was one like Joshua's army? What if believers said, "Your victory is my victory," "I am with you," "Stay encouraged," and "Let's love our cities together"? As this happens, the world sees witness that Jesus was sent by God.

Jesus expects the church to walk in love toward one another. This calls for different ethnic groups learning to work together. Many of the challenges of cooperation and working together are made much easier when we consider thems to be us-es. As Jesus saw it, all those who do the Father's will are family. The children of Israel corrected their selfish request and made sure their desires included God's plan for all Israel.

Do your plans for the body of Christ include non-palace believers from other ethnic groups? If not, you can change the way you pray today.

If we pray like Jesus taught us to pray and receive the truth that in Christ, we are one family with one mission, we will be able to more quickly overcome many of the underlying challenges that make it difficult for different ethnic groups and wealth classes to work together.

Rethink "greater" and "better"

Comparison, pride, and jealousy produce tension and division. In the family of Jesus, our different giftings and strengths should not lead to these things. When everyone does their part, we should produce a greater blessing and better results than we would on our own. Working together is the right idea according to 1 Corinthians 12, but it is fair to ask why isn't this happening to a greater degree already?

Because the underlying tension between us and them is who is better and who is greater (John 4:12). We hear this idea come out when the Samaritan woman at the well asks Jesus, "Are you greater than our father Jacob?" And then she asked, "Is the water better?" The issue between ethnic groups is who is greater and who is better. Whose people are greater, whose products are better, ours or theirs?

The beautiful thing about the community that Jesus builds is that he has no problem acknowledging those who carry greater gifts or those who make a better product. Jesus is so secure in himself that he can celebrate the greater things that come from others.

This is why he highlighted moments when Samaritans showed greater character than Jews—his Jewishness was never intimidated by this truth. It was an opportunity for him to help shift the mind-sets of his palace disciples who were Jews.

How well do you celebrate others in the family of God? Who could you celebrate that would expect you to be in competition with them?

We will remain divided if we see the greater gifts and the better products of others as a sign of their value with envy and jealousy (James 3:13-18). Who is better or greater isn't a helpful question. A better question is: What is our purpose together?

Jesus told his disciples, who were obviously not greater than him, that they would do greater works. This is the mentality that helps people walk as one. When I look at you, I'm looking to discover how God wants to use you. I want to hear what you believe God wants you to do in your life, at your school, in your organization, and in your family. I'm looking to see how I may be a part of encouraging or supporting your achievement of his greater purposes in your life. Your success could be the difference in someone's life and family being changed for generations.

Jesus was great because he fulfilled his assignment and pushed others toward theirs without comparison or jealousy. He gave us a model for how to work as one. He would die for our sins and do the part that no one else could do. While he lived, he served his disciples and prepared them to do their part. That's the concept of what it means to be greater in the Kingdom. It is to serve others, not to compete.

The greater one in the Kingdom is the one who serves. The greater one in the kingdom is the one who is thankful for your success in Christ. When we find someone that does something better, it is our opportunity to learn from one another.

When Mary and her sons felt like their voice was greater than the followers of Jesus in the room that he was speaking to, Jesus explained what heaven was really like, that all have the possibility, the opportunity to be great in the Kingdom of God regardless of who they are or who their parents are, or whether they are a certain ethnicity, bloodline, or family.

The doers of God's will have the same opportunity to be honored, please God, and be rewarded in the eternal kingdom. Flesh and blood give no advantage in the Kingdom of Heaven. Skin color gives no advantage in the Kingdom of Heaven. Even Jesus's natural family would receive no advantage in the Kingdom of Heaven. Everyone would be judged for their own obedience and for doing the will of the Father.

How can two people of different ethnic groups work together with so many fears and subtle slights? We would have to take the same position that Jesus did. Jesus knew his assignment, and he knew what was on the Father's heart. Jesus knew that his assignment was to be a bridge of reconciliation for all humankind, not just the Jews.

Therefore, he made sure that during his life he set an example of showing that ethnicity did not prevail over submission to God's will. He made a point of being intentional to make opportunities for divided communities to come together and be in the same space. He made a point to use his influence over his followers and lead his disciples into spaces outside of their palace communities.

The Samaritans probably did not know their value, but Jesus did, and he treated them according to the value that the Father had placed on them, so that they too would be respected and walk in the things of God and be part of his family. If we walk like Jesus, we are helping people become "greater" and know their value even more because of how we treat them.

What does it look like for us to have rich relationships across ethnic groups? When it is genuine and when we have taken the time to grow in esteem toward one another (free of offense), relationship is more natural. When our hearts are healthy and we are for one another, we start boasting about what the other one brings to the table.

I've seen it. I saw a community of pastors from Austin, Texas, who were practicing this. In this instance, one was White, the other was Black, and they had both been a part of a commitment to pray together as pastors for the city of Austin for several years. When they heard these teachings, they were amazed and locked in conversation for several minutes. You could tell from a distance that they were having a rich conversation, so I went and joined them to listen and learn. As soon as I joined them, they began to share with me by talking about one another. I don't remember them introducing themselves. They introduced each other.

I don't think they realized what they were doing, but the first thing out of each of their mouths was boasting about who the other man was and how his life was so full of grace, how appreciative they were of one another, and just how much love and respect they had for each other. As soon as one finished, the other jumped in, and they went back and forth for two or three minutes.

This was authentic and from the heart. This was a result of leaders who chose to commit to praying together as fellow pastors in the city, who came from different worlds, different backgrounds, and different experiences but who love the same God. This can be true across any ethnic divide for neighbors, coworkers, classmates and those in a city who are seeking to show the love of God to their cities and spheres of influence.

We all can do and experience these things. This is the direction Jesus desires for all of us.

Chapter 9

Jesus Made His Values Clear I Make Your Values Clear

9 o'clock

> *"'But the time is coming—indeed it's here now—when true worshippers will worship the Father in spirit and in truth. The Father is looking for those who will worship him that way. For God is Spirit, so those who worship him must worship in spirit and in truth.'" John 4:23-24*

Your values matter – In 2020, in the United States of America, two stories dominated news headlines—the deaths of Ahmaud Arbery and George Floyd. Two Black men were killed by White men. One was killed by a father and son who claimed to be policing their neighborhood. The other was killed by a police officer who was answering a complaint about him using a counterfeit $20 bill. Dissenting views on guilt and innocence flooded the airwaves for weeks, riots broke out, and relationships were challenged within families, workspaces, and churches. Two hashtags began dominating social media—#bluelivesmatter and #blacklivesmatter. People asked: Whose side are you on? Which hashtag do you support?

Most people felt the pressure to use one hashtag or the other. Seeing the turmoil that pastors, business owners, organization leaders, and people in general had to face, I offered a different set of advice. It brought relief to many leaders and families who could not fully communicate their care for both groups by using one or the other hashtag. My advice was, "Use your own words and make *your* values clear."

Jesus pointed to the Father

The Sermon on the Mount in Matthew 5-7 is a brilliant set of instructions and a necessary part of us being able to live out a lifestyle that doesn't reflect the divisions of the culture. It also shows us that it's necessary to make our values clear.

How can the world know we love them when they don't know us?

How can strangers know we welcome them or want to invite them if when they look at our lives, they can only judge us by our skin color, context, and the palace rumors they've heard about people who look like us, vote like us, and live in whatever communities we live in? All others can do is judge the outside of our cups if we don't make our values known and clear.

Jesus made his values clear in the Sermon on the Mount, where he redefined fulfillment and what pleases God. You can read different versions of the Sermon on the Mount for yourself and discover how it opens with a declaration of values called the Beatitudes. You'll see countercultural truths and expectations being declared.

For example, Jesus said, "God blesses those who are poor in spirit and realize their need for him. Theirs is the Kingdom of Heaven" (Matthew 5:3). There's more value in being approachable than in winning arguments and having the last say. Being a listener allows us to love others better. There is more of the Kingdom of Heaven shown through the life of the humble than the proud. Jesus also said, "God blesses those who mourn, for they will be comforted" (Matthew 5:4). There's value in being touched with the pain of this world and offering it to God instead of avoiding pain and being out-of-reach from those in need.

Values matter. God's values are different from the world's values. What he celebrates and what those who love the world celebrate are different. Jesus sets our focus, so we don't expect the wrong things in life—like pain-free, problem-free living. The Beatitudes help us live joyfully with healthy expectations in a world of pain and disappointment. Jesus directs our attention to what the Father values, so we are clear about how he sees things.

Graciously affirm what you believe

When society gets in an uproar and puts fear and division out as the strongest narrative, people begin to question one another, and mistrust prevails. This is not the time to go silent. This also isn't the time to defend yourself and your palace. It's a time to declare your values with words.

Why let others guess what you think or put words in your mouth? Why let your skin color, wealth status, political party, or anything else speak for you? If the position of these groups doesn't fully reflect Jesus and if any of these groups' most vocal leaders are speaking in a way that is divisive and condescending, then their character and position could easily be attributed to you.

Do like Jesus. Use your words and voice to let others know what to expect from you. The ways of Jesus are countercultural to where the world stands. We can't expect a narrative of forgiveness, peace-making, and bold love for our enemies to be what people expect to receive from us if we don't make our values clear.

In Matthew 5:9, Jesus made it clear that God blesses those who work for peace because they will be called the children of God. In the world, those who work for peace are often misrepresented as compromisers or those who won't take a stand. Jesus took a stand, but he also worked for peace. He took a stand even when his life was on the line.

It's not an easy thing to work for peace. It's much easier to simply stay in our palaces and use the excuse that the world is bad, and nothing will change. But we are so thankful that Jesus came into our world and our brokenness. The way he handled ethnic division made an impact. He changed how history viewed Samaritans. The results of his intentional response were proof that God blesses those who work for peace, calling them the children of God.

There are times we must verbalize our values. When anger and bitterness prevail, people may seem like they have forgotten every good moment we ever had together. In fact, some of the very people we've handled without partiality and sacrificed for may rise to question us or even turn against us. It's not personal.

Jesus didn't take it personally when the Samaritan woman at the well brought up the racial issues between them. He proceeded to communicate his values and who he was without the slightest concern for her seeing him as just another one of them. Jesus wasted no time showing her that she was seen, respected, and worth a conversation. This won her attention and her heart. If you get offended because someone is misjudging or offended at you, how can you make things better? In the spaces where we lead and influence, regardless of how others respond, we can make sure that every ethnic group is welcome, seen, and treated with dignity.

Sharing our values is like making a commercial to sell our product. It's not the best idea to make a long commercial that condemns every other kind of product so that people will want to buy yours. The real secret is to make people understand why your product is good. Be careful not to spend so much time condemning the values of others instead of declaring and showing the greater values of heaven.

Show the world that there is a love that is greater than offense and animosity. Show that you care about others with your speech, time, hospitality, and presence. Be visible, reachable, and relatable outside of your palace ethnic group and wealth class by serving, solving problems, and meeting real needs.

Celebrate what you are for

Let your voice be raised high. Why be timid over the idea of loving others? Celebrate and promote your values in a way that others can hear you, your family, or your organization. Throw out any confusion and silence any questions by boldly rejecting strife and seeking to love more. Sacrificing for others and showing up in spaces where people have a need are values to declare loudly.

Without these celebrations and declarations, many others may miss the opportunity to join you in practicing and promoting healthy values. The Samaritan woman was so impacted by Jesus that she went and told the whole city to come see him. She celebrated so widely that a harvest of Samaritans came and believed in Jesus.

This was the same woman who was likely belittled in her community because she had had five husbands. But she didn't let her past or how people saw her hinder her from sharing with them the good news of what she had discovered. If this woman who carried the cultural shame of five painful and broken marriages could let go of her yesterday, lift her voice, and point everyone to Jesus, then we can too. "Come see a man" was her gathering cry as she left Jesus and went throughout her town calling others to him. She had found a better way with hope-filled values, and she was not hiding or being timid about it.

Is it a point of celebration for you to realize that Jesus's answer to race was to show up, be present, receive "them," and invite them into the beauty of God's community and way of doing things? Is it a point of celebration for you to realize that the Samaritans were never an afterthought for him and that he fully wanted his Jewish followers to be prepared to receive them as part of God's family? It was to the Samaritan woman.

She learned that in God's eyes the day of division was over. The divide between Jews and Samaritans about whose mountain to worship on was now an obsolete point and now any worshipper (Jew, Samaritan, or other) who worshipped him in spirit and truth would be among those God would seek. This was enough for the Samaritan woman to not need an evangelism class or a lesson on being a witness before she took off and told everyone she could find about Jesus, a man with a better way.

When we speak of celebrating and putting our values out there, it could be by putting words and phrases on the walls of your home, car, front door, workspace, email signature, clothes, or social media posts. The world builds community around dissatisfaction. God builds community around hope.

It's easy to talk about the things we dislike about one another. It's easy to join the palace conversations and speak about all the negatives about the thems. But Jesus is our countercultural leader. He set an example of celebrating the values he wanted to see more of. This is why he told the story of the one leper who returned to give thanks as showing the value he wanted to see more of—gratitude. He made it clear that this healed leper was a Samaritan. Once again, he was celebrating Samaritans, using them as models of character and virtue.

Jesus was wise in his response to race, and we should be too. He didn't respond to their division by rallying Samaritans against the Jews or by name-calling. It's easy to complain and allow our dissatisfaction to drive our conversations but murmuring and complaining caused a generation of the children of Israel to not enter the promised land. Jesus sets an example of celebrating our values over complaining about the things we don't like.

When we create spaces or events that promote our values in public, let's not be shy. If division can have the microphone and bring misery and unrest on everyone, why wouldn't bridge-building and peacemaking be honored even more? Consider inviting with a public invitation those who don't look like you. Consider creating the kinds of spaces and celebrations that aren't happening in the world.

Let people see that our freedom to love beyond our ethnic groups and wealth classes is simply following what Jesus modeled and taught. It's not easy to bridge ethnic divides, but let's not let the difficulty of doing right encourage us to fall into condescending and negative attacks that don't help us reach tomorrow.

Proverbs 24:17-18 says, "Don't rejoice when your enemies fall; don't be happy when they stumble. For the Lord will be displeased with you and will turn his anger away from them." It's true that others commit sins. It may be true that the thems you despise have some sinful behaviors. But be careful. This proverb says that God will deal with them, but he may also stop punishing them because of your pleasure at seeing them punished. Celebrating the downfall of others is not godly behavior.

Beware of campaigns that are driven by hurt and watch out if you find yourself saying, "I'm going to get even with them, if it's the last thing I do." Instead, if we wrap God's grace around our heart, he will be the one to vindicate us if needed. Either grace will fill our hearts or bitterness. Which will we choose? It's hard for a person who is offended and angry to be someone who produces healing and reconciliation.

It's hard to celebrate values and invite other ethnic groups when you won't release others through forgiveness. This posture is self-defeating. It's hard to publicly put your values out there for all to see when you still want to see the other group suffer for something they've done to you. This doesn't negate the pain, but the Bible is clear that bitterness springs up only to defile many (Hebrews 12:15). There is no reconciliation or healing in bitterness. We are not only called to do right, but we are called to release those who do us wrong.

No matter how much labor we put into having conversations, creating spaces, and bridging divides, we won't last, and we won't finish if anger, bitterness, and offense prevail in our hearts. It's like a hole in the fuel tank. It's like a rusted-out engine. The fuel will leak out, and we'll barely be able to get out of the driveway. To do the works that Jesus did, we understand that there is no ministry of reconciliation without first comprehending that we need forgiveness ourselves and second that it's our privilege to forgive others.

This takes us to the cross of Jesus. If we want to walk like Jesus, then we must come to where Jesus did when he hung on the cross: he fully forgave. The Bible calls us to forgive from the heart. From the cross, Jesus said, "Father, forgive them, for they know not what they do" (Luke 23:34). Jesus is the one who gives light. We also can pray, "Father, I forgive others, for they know not what they do."

Chapter 10

Jesus Embraced the Father's Plan | Embrace God's Dream

10 o'clock

> "But those who drink the water I give will never be thirsty again. It becomes a fresh, bubbling spring within them, giving them eternal life." John 4:14

Dream boldly – Dr. Martin Luther King Jr. stood at the Lincoln Memorial and challenged all of America with his famous "I have a dream" speech. His dream was bold, personal, generational and specific.

> Bold – "the sons of former slaves and the sons of former slave owners will be able to sit down together at the table of brotherhood."

> Personal – "my four little children will one day live in a nation where they will not be judged by the color of their skin but by the content of their character."

> Generational and Specific – "one day right down in Alabama little black boys and black girls will be able to join hands with little white boys and white girls as sisters and brothers."

A dream that is cautious and unclear is no dream at all. Dreaming requires courage and the ability to see beyond your pain. Since we know that John17:21 is the desire of Jesus, we cannot let pain and offense hinder us from communicating bold, personal, generational and specific pictures of being one.

Who is right?

Just as much as there is a right and a wrong way to handle pain, there is a right and a wrong way to discover the real problem. When two sides are at odds, even in a marriage, if the driving question is, "Who is right?" then it may take a while to bring peace to the situation. Starting the process of peacemaking with the right question is important. We will never reach reconciliation and unity by asking, "Who is right?" and "Who is wrong?"

A better focus is, "What is the solution?" The "Who is right?" question is easily a setup for accusation and blame. If we dig a little deeper, the "Who is right?" question is seeking to tell the other group, "You are the problem! I'm right, you're wrong, and you need to listen to me." No wonder arguments get stuck with this approach. Focusing on solutions invites insight and contribution toward identifying a path forward.

The Samaritan woman at the well posed a "Who is right?" question to Jesus when she asked, "Who is right about which mountain people should worship on?" Jesus knew the Jews were "right" about where to worship, but he also knew that the answer was to focus on a solution that brought them together. The woman's question was setting up one group or the other to feel greater and look down on the other. Instead, Jesus wraps his answer in the solution and refuses to label one group as right and the other as the problem.

Pay close attention to how Jesus responded to the woman in John 4:

> "Believe me, dear woman, the time is coming when it will no longer matter whether you worship the Father on this mountain or in Jerusalem.[21] You Samaritans know very little about the one you worship, while we Jews know all about him, for salvation comes through the Jews.[22] But the time is coming – indeed it's here now – when the true worshippers will worship the Father in spirit and in truth. The Father is looking for those who will worship him that way."[23]

Jesus did not start by identifying who was right and who was wrong. He pointed to the Father's plan to seek sincere worshippers from every ethnic group. He could have just shared verse 22, that the Jews are right and Samaritans are wrong, but that statement doesn't carry the hope, promise, and invitation to the Father's plans. If Jesus had only said verse 22, then we could keep telling others that we're right. But he didn't. He opened with verse 21 and closed with verse 23, with the fuller perspective of what the Father desires.

What a lesson in how to talk to one another! This way makes room for us-es and thems to team up and address problems together. Even if we are right about something, according to Jesus there is no badge of honor in making sure to let the thems know they are wrong. The healthy focus is on God's plan, which is being one in spirit and in truth.

When we live to reflect the Father's plans, we are not wrapped up in condemning others or justifying ourselves. Being mature in Christ means aligning our aims with the Father's. Every interaction we have is to build toward God's desire for the followers of Jesus to be one.

What Jesus models for us in this us-them conversation helps us guard our hearts when we are making a point. Proof that we are right about something is not revealed by our ability to prove someone else wrong. A greater measure is showing our ability to communicate God's best without frustration or a focus on justifying ourselves (or our palace group).

Being like Jesus is being able to focus on the goal of walking as one in spirit and truth. Anyone can walk with their palace community. Anyone can stir up a palace conversation and complain about how wrong the thems are, but Jesus's followers are called to usher others (and ourselves) into a greater tomorrow through humility, truthfulness, and grace. Jesus spoke the truth directly, but he wrapped truth in an invitation to a greater tomorrow.

When we make our points about race are our tone, focus, and words inviting others into a better tomorrow or are we just proving ourselves right? Do the points we make carry an excitement and hope about God's best?

We have discussed how Jesus answered the Samaritan woman's questions at the well. She believed that the problem was that they needed to know who was right. But Jesus looked at the problem and understood that the solution was less about figuring out who was right and more about understanding God's beautiful plans for an end to ethnic division and an invitation to those who will worship in spirit and in truth. The real problem was that neither Jews nor Samaritans were fully aware about what the Father was intending and how the new tomorrow of no walls of strife between ethnic groups was beginning with Jesus.

Solving race issues is not just about how we respond—or fail to respond—to pain, but it is coming into agreement with how God sees the situation. This then becomes a foundation for joyful collaboration, like the Samaritan woman gave Jesus.

Learning from a dreamer

There was a man named Joseph, a dreamer. God gave him dreams of his future when he was young. His brothers hated him, rejected him, and sold him into slavery. Despite his situation, he still gave his best as a slave and did whatever he could to make things better for others, so much so that Potiphar, his master, soon entrusted him with the full stewardship of his house, business, and finances.

Later, when Joseph was falsely accused by Potiphar's wife of sexual harassment, he was thrown into prison. Once again, having been dealt the hard blow of betrayal, he still gave his best and offered solutions in the prison and was ultimately raised up to be the chief steward of the prison.

In another turn of events, Joseph was called upon by Pharoah, king of Egypt, to interpret a dream and help solve a national problem. Joseph gave the interpretation and a solution for how to address the national crisis. He went from slavery to prison to second-in-command of all of Egypt as God gave him favor.

Joseph somehow never let his pain and disappointment stop him from giving his best and making things better for others in every situation he faced. He always came up with solutions that brought peace and prosperity.

You would expect a man, who was forsaken by his own brothers and trapped in an Egyptian slave system to be depressed and struggle to have hope. You would expect him to think God must be against him. But Joseph didn't. He faithfully gave his best, offered solutions, and made things better for others in every circumstance until his God-dream became reality. God even brought reconciliation between Joseph and his brothers.

How do we carry the God-dream, the Father's best plans? I'm talking about the things that seem impossible, but we choose to pray and believe anyway. I'm talking about the things that we are to pray that "his kingdom come and his will be done on earth as it is in heaven" (Matthew 6:10). These are the things that cause us to walk in faith.

Abraham had a God-dream of being the father of many nations, even though his wife was barren, and they were aging. Jesus had a God-dream of his followers being one. Believing the Father's plans leads us to live by faith, so that our actions and responses to one another aren't driven by our pain but by his promise.

What would happen if the pain of today and yesterday lost power over the John 17:21 dream of what tomorrow could be? Joseph's response to pain gives us a picture of what it might look like. If our dreams are God's dreams, then we can be confident that God sees us, hears us, and will bring about his best plans far beyond what we can "ask or think" (Ephesians 3:20). Jesus shows us how to respond to the Father's plans instead of reacting to touchy, painful, and often personal race issues. The one who looks to God for results will have peace, conquer bitterness, and have the ability to respond with grace.

Dream with God

The saddest situation is to go through the sufferings of this life and have only bitterness and offense to show for it. Joseph refused to let that be his story, and God brought restoration in his life. We too are called to know and carry God's dreams by faith.

I believe the dreams of God were expressed in John 17:20-23. It's important to be able to see God's plan and make his dreams ours. I'm not talking about coming up with our own dreams and asking God to bless them. That's not what Jesus taught. However, we may be confident of God's help and assistance when our dreams come from his desires. If we align our dreams with his, we can move mountains.

Joseph shows us that no circumstance is too great for God. He shows us we should give our best, make things better, and offer solutions to help others in every situation we face without falling prey to bitterness and offense. This is how to make the Father's plans, the God-dreams, a reality.

It's only through God's plan that we have a path to forgiveness. Receiving Jesus is a platform where sins can be confessed and forgiven. It opens the door for people to begin living in the new kingdom of freedom and life.

Following Jesus's and Joseph's examples shows us that we don't have to wait for others to like us or agree with the way Jesus handled race before we put these principles into practice. The response of others doesn't stop us from greeting the those outside their palace communities, enjoying their cultures, inviting them into our homes, learning their stories from them, serving their communities for their success, introducing them to our palace friends, and partnering with them to shine the light of Christ.

The Father's solution to ethnic division is Jesus and how to get there was modeled through his life. The Father's plan was clear. The Jews would learn Jesus's ways, and they would begin to live like Jesus lived. Then after Jesus rose from the dead, he told them to be witnesses in Jerusalem, Judea, Samaria, and to the ends of the earth (Acts 1:8).

Handling Pain

In this life, pain is a reality. It can be blinding. It can leave us knowing the truth in our mind, but then being unable to bend our will to do what Jesus did and follow his commands. If we let it, pain can convince us that the only proper response to being disappointed, misunderstood, or handled unfairly is to get even or finish this life taking care of ourselves and distrusting others. Pain can leave us bitter and lacking hope.

If pain is this powerful, what is the solution? The first step is to admit that a lack of hope and bitterness is a sign of an incomplete perspective. In other words, we must begin by making a simple confession, "I'm handling this in the wrong way. This is not what Jesus would do." If I were handling this situation as Jesus would, then the fruit of love, joy, peace, patience, and kindness would be in my heart and show in my words when I talk about or see "them."

Some think that getting even is the way to deal with a people group that has hurt them but getting even will never produce God's plans. Joseph did not get even; he gave his best and offered solutions. Some have given up the God-dream of Christians being one because the promise seems so impossible. But growing cold toward others and being filled with distrust is not the path to fulfilling God's plans.

Pain can make us lean wholly on God. We are reminded that we fall short, but God is faithful. We get to choose whether the disappointment of others or our hope in God will mold our hearts. If disappointment wins, how could we ever give our best like Joseph and despite our circumstances remain postured to see the God-dream, the Father's best plans, become reality?

We are talking about the pain of division. The pain in Jesus's day was that the Jews' interpretation of handling "unclean" Samaritans was to treat them as invisible. It was to do what is usually done in us-them divides and not say anything good about them, refuse to drink or eat in the same places, and definitely not spend time in one another's homes.

Division, distance, and animosity are born out of pain and offense. Healthy relationships, hope, and the Father's best plans are birthed from living in the hope of God's promises like Joseph did. Jesus responded to ethnic division by focusing on the Father's plans.

Most of the time, we are responding to ethnic division by the pain or lack of pain it causes us. If the lack of unity has caused us pain, we respond with great zeal and passion. If the lack of unity has not caused us pain, we lack zeal and even small efforts feel laborious.

Jesus didn't base his zeal for this conversation on the presence or absence of personal pain the division between Jews and Samaritans caused him. He tore down walls and created a brilliant solution because it was the Father's plan.

There is nothing wrong with discovering solutions because a situation has caused us personal pain. It's noble to get involved and care for others (like the good Samaritan did) when we see something causing another pain, but to be pure in heart and see what God is doing, we must move from the motivation of pain to being motivated by discovering the Father's plan and what is on his heart.

Chapter 11

Jesus Changed Narratives by Telling Their Stories | Share Their Stories

11 o'clock

> *"Then a despised Samaritan came along, and when he saw the man, he felt compassion for him." Luke 10:33*

A Barnabas Leader – Leading local news stations was his career for over two decades, but it was now coming to a close. John looked out into his future and was okay with the challenge of the unknown. He had given his life to Jesus and become a part of Wes' community of leaders who were working together to make a difference. He was continually experiencing the power of walking and dreaming with God.

When John heard this message at one of our Bridge Conferences, he was convinced that everyone needed to handle the race conversation in the same way, free of bitterness and, in his terms, free of vitriol. He called every former relationship that he could think of from radio to the major local news stations and told them about our non-toxic way of handling conversations on race. His zeal to tell our stories brought us into the offices of Oklahoma's media leaders. They also were passionate about making sure that stories were shared in a way that was not fueling division and were excited about working together to make a difference.

With his New York accent and his new faith, John made a difference. We found ourselves sharing our story with his palace community of media because of John's commitment to "share their story." Just like Barnabas used his influence and connections to help launch the message and ministry of Paul, John shared our story with those we would have never met, so that healthier conversations around race would prevail on the local news.

Jesus made "them" the heroes

Jesus changes the narrative on race by telling their stories. We can impact the conversation about race in our world too by following his example.

In the story of the Good Samaritan, Jesus is teaching on the second greatest commandment: love your neighbor as yourself. Millions, maybe billions, have heard this story over the past 2,000 years. It's powerful because in John 8 we find the Jews, those from Jesus's palace community, contending with him for an extended amount of time. They get so angry at him that they even call him an illegitimate child.

They wanted to call him names that would hurt. When those words neither hurt nor swayed him, they tried to find the most harmful and disrespectful name they could use by calling him a Samaritan and a devil (John 8:48). In that time, calling someone a Samaritan was almost the same as using the n-word in America. It was a derogatory term, a racial slur. It was something to imply that a person was worthless and a curse to society.

So in Jesus's day, being called a Samaritan was a put-down. Today, in America, it's a compliment to be called a Good Samaritan. Who changed this narrative? Jesus did. Who changed the way history would think of the Samaritans? Jesus did.

This is a powerful truth. Jesus lifted the sting of who the Samaritans were by his own wisdom and authority. If it were up to the Jews in Jesus's palace community, everyone in history would still be using "Samaritan" as a derogatory term. But now it is a compliment.

When Jesus sought to build his church, the people before whom the gates of hell would not prevail, he used stories. He carefully selected stories that would strengthen the church if they could hear what he said and follow his example. If we did an objective tally of the stories Jesus shared, we would find that his stories mostly celebrated the faith, character, spiritual hunger, and responses of non-palace people, so we all would be provoked to greater things.

Jesus knew the stories he told would set the tone for how generations would follow him throughout time, so he was intentional about who he honored as the heroes of his stories. He celebrated the widow's offering over the gifts of the rich. He honored the Samaritan's reflection of loving a neighbor over the behavior of the Jewish religious leaders. He showed Lazarus, the poor beggar, being carried by the angels into paradise with Abraham at his death. He showed the rich man lifting his eyes in hell, begging for a drop of water to touch his tongue.

When Jesus told stories of earthly wealth, he highlighted moments when the rich responded to God without calculating their losses, like Zacchaeus the tax collector did when he repented for cheating people. These were all stories that highlighted acts of faith and character rarely celebrated in divided palace communities.

There were a thousand stories Jesus could have told, but he chose the stories of the weak things to confound the mighty and the despised things to bring to nothing the things the world considers important. This choice of stories was no accident. He intentionally chose to esteem another ethnic community over his own. This doesn't mean he hated his own people group, but he rejected blinding arrogance and was willing to also appreciate and celebrate the thems.

Look for solutions outside your palace

Jesus didn't come to spread the attitudes of the palace community.

He came to spread the Kingdom of God. Jesus wasn't on earth to continue the blindness in people's hearts or misrepresent the Father. Jesus was on earth to bring the kingdom and the ways of heaven to us. He was strategic about how he talked about Samaritans. In the story of the Good Samaritan, he made the thems look better than the us.

This very idea is offensive to the palace mind. Could they be our teachers? Are they showing the character of Christ in greater ways than us? The palace mind wouldn't think to look outside their community for answers, solutions, encouragement, or direction. But 1 Corinthians 12 says, "We need one another." What are we missing as the body of Christ on earth by claiming that we don't need one another? This idea is in direct opposition to what the Scriptures say.

In Philippians 2:3, the Apostle Paul says, "Don't be selfish; don't try to impress others. Be humble, thinking of others as better than yourselves." Does this apply to how we should see people in other ethnic groups, or does this mean that the only people esteemed as better than us can be those from our palace community?

It's amazing how palace thinking can even impact the way we read the Scriptures. When the Bible says love your neighbor, the palace mind only thinks about its own ethnic group. When the Bible says esteem others better than yourselves, the palace mind only thinks about esteeming those in its own palace community.

How long could racial issues last if just this one Scripture were practiced in the body of Christ? We could be the best at listening to one another and learning from one another. There are treasures, solutions, and God-ideas waiting outside of our ethnic groups and wealth classes.

"God chose things the world considers foolish in order to shame those who think they are wise. And he chose things that are power-less to shame those who are powerful. God chose things despised by the world, things counted as nothing at all, and used them to bring to nothing what the world considers important. As a result, no one can ever boast in the presence of God" (1 Corinthians 1:27-29).

Pharoah sat in his Egyptian palace facing a challenge he had not dealt with before. God had given him a dream that he knew was se-rious, but he didn't know what it meant. He didn't have anyone serv-ing him that could give him a correct interpretation of his dream. What would Pharoah do? There were no answers in the palace, and this was serious.

Eventually, Pharoah's cupbearer remembered someone from out-side their palace community and ethnic group who could interpret the dream. There was someone who had survived slavery and prison and had a phenomenal gift to bring wisdom, solutions, and inter-pret dreams. His name was Joseph. They had crossed paths when the cupbearer was falsely accused (just like Joseph, but for a dif-ferent reason) and ended up in the same prison, where Joseph had accurately interpreted the cupbearer's dream. The cupbearer could tell those in the palace of Joseph's ability because he had personally experienced Joseph's abilities in his own time of need.

The cupbearer spoke up, and Pharoah reached outside his (literal) palace community. Joseph brought answers, and God brought grace and mercy to the land of Egypt and surrounding nations through Jo-seph's warning and wisdom. Egypt survived a worldwide famine and was positioned to feed those who came from surrounding nations for help. There was a solution outside the palace, outside Egypt's ethnic group, and outside Pharoah's wealth class.

Thank God that Joseph never submitted to the pain of the rejection and betrayal in his life and kept living as one who would eventually be remembered by God. Thank God the cupbearer told the story of Joseph's great character and ability to his palace community. The source of great grace and a faith that can reach a city (like the Samaritan woman) is often found in those the world has trained us to overlook and despise.

Tell their stories

When we see prejudice in our palace communities, we may want to stand on a platform or find a media outlet and rebuke everyone. Maybe we think about how we should "have a talk" with our relative who uses racial slurs. There is a place for direct confrontation, like when Paul confronted Peter and when Jesus rebuked his disciples for their harshness in asking to call down fire from heaven on the Samaritans.

But remember that Jesus packaged his truth in a lifestyle and heart that carried no offense. Instead of edgy zeal, try counteracting ignorance by promoting and sharing stories in the palace that are beautiful in God's eyes. Try telling stories of the non-palace friends and communities that you've learned.

Be careful not to confront ignorance and blindness with anger couched as righteous indignation. We all have blindness toward ethnic groups that we simply don't know much about. We don't know their social cues, codes of honor, greetings, and social expectations. In addition to our own ignorance, we've probably formed an opinion about them based on things we value. There are the inherited beliefs, outside media sources, and personal interpretations of what we think they believe that further derail our ability to relate to them. This is why we need stories, true stories, and stories of celebration that can help us understand who they are and how to connect.

Use the weapon of stories. Use the building material that Jesus uses to strengthen his church. Our palace worlds are built out of stories that cause us to believe one thing or another. In order to bring about the Father's plan for us to be one, learn and share the stories of our brothers and sisters who are not in our ethnic groups and wealth classes. We are changing the narrative when we tell these stories in our palace worlds.

This is what practicing Jesus's ways can do. We may not be the light of the whole world, but we are called to be a light in our world (meaning our palaces, the spaces we influence). We can create opportunities through the stories we tell in order to allow opportunity for people to change how they view ethnic groups that they currently despise.

We are the salt of the earth. We change the flavor of situations. We are the light of the world. We intentionally tell stories that bring understanding. We tell stories that expose darkness and makes things clearer. We refuse to stay compromisingly silent and let dark conversations about others prevail in spaces where we could be sharing better stories about "them."

We are called to obey Jesus and model his lifestyle. We are yeast in spaces where people don't even regard the name of Jesus. Yeast has a way of causing the whole loaf to rise. We are in our families and workspaces to model love and healthy conversations that rise above evil talk, racial slurs, and negative jokes about others. Let your character and conversation change the way your circles of relationships talk about "them."

This brings about a powerful challenge for everyone who follows Jesus. We may no longer hide behind our personality types or fears when we have the power to make things better for everyone. We can be peacemakers by simply celebrating their stories in palace spaces like Jesus did.

How could you use your influence to change the way others see the people who would be considered Samaritans by your palace community? If we want to know what impact our lives should have in toxic and divisive environments, we must respect the fact that Jesus changed the narrative on a whole ethnic group. We can change narratives too.

Jesus knew that much of the Jews' and Samaritans' animosity and division toward each other was based on ignorance. If they knew God's plans, they would have grace toward others. Racial issues are not all intentional, and the evil and slights are not all done in malice. Many are done in ignorance. People have been raised in environments that either spoke down about others or didn't acknowledge or esteem them at all. Even those who have deep hatred and who seek harm to other ethnic groups operate out of ignorance. It's hard to celebrate and respect what we don't know.

Jesus recognized that the value of the Samaritans needed to be raised in the eyes of the Jews. He also recognized how sharing the story of Samaritans, a group his palace community despised, would motivate his fellow Jews. If Samaritans were the ones who demonstrated the right way, then what is that saying about a Jew who claims to know God still not going out of their comfort zone to love their neighbors? Jesus showed his wisdom by intentionally promoting the poor, overlooked, non-palace people as the heroes of his stories.

We have the power to practice this too. The thing that brings momentum in the Kingdom of God and causes God's people to move is when we tell the right stories. When we tell stories of sacrifice, everyone can go and do the same in proportion to what they have. When we only tell stories of the rich and the powerful, it may not be a sin, but it also may not be the best thing.

In some cases, when someone has given thousands of dollars, others will only think about the fact that they're having trouble paying their bills, so maybe the rich person should just help them too because their little gift won't make a difference anyway. The widow's two mites seemed insignificant until Jesus took the opportunity to teach his disciples about what God values, saying the rich give "out of their abundance," but the widow gave "more than them all." "More than" in heaven is not based on quantity but proportion. The story is used as an invitation for everyone to give sacrificially, regardless of whether the world has made them feel greater or less than others because of their wealth or ethnicity.

When we value what Jesus values, we recognize that heaven celebrates gifts that are proportional. Then when we hear the story of someone who has less and still gives like the widow, we recognize that if the widow could give, we all can give.

Chapter 12

Jesus Knew the Value of His Story | Share Your Story

12 o'clock

> *"Then Jesus told her, 'I am the Messiah!'"*
> *John 4:26*

A Passion for Being One – There are some people in the world that seem like they shine just a little brighter because of their freedom and welcoming personalities. That is Kimm. She was like a modern-day Samaritan woman in her zeal to share unity in Jesus, but white, Suburban, and middle-class. Few people carried her zeal for being a part of a new narrative around unity in the body of Christ. She and her husband Jim left the comfort of their palace church community and friends to join a small and powerful church in the black community over thirty minutes away.

With a simple faith and the gift of music, she also started "Know Your Neighbor". In the living rooms of her palace friends, she would bring "us" and "them" together around worship and storytelling. She would share her story and how God was teaching her about loving her neighbors and she made invitation for others to discover what they could do in their lives and worlds to be a part of a better narrative around race – a Jesus narrative. Many people respond to Jesus, but some motivate us all with the way they run after God's dreams with all of their heart, soul and mind. Kimm used her story and her light without reservation and made a difference.

Jesus shared his story

Jesus knew the value of his story. He shared his story with the Samaritan woman at the well, which caused her to run and tell the story to others.

The Samaritan woman also knew the value of her story. She, a Samaritan, had just been treated by this Jewish man with love and grace, even when her past was exposed. And she hadn't just encountered any Jewish man, but it was Jesus, who revealed himself to her as the Messiah! So we can understand why she ran and told everyone about how her mundane trip to the well became an encounter with heaven.

Jesus had said to her, "If you only knew the gift God has for you and who you are speaking to, you would ask me, and I would give you living water" (John 4:10).

"If you only knew" is Jesus's response to the Samaritan woman because he knew what he had to offer her. I want to give that Samaritan woman a high-five for not missing her opportunity to follow God's way! She had so many opportunities to be offended, but she focused on Jesus.

When Jesus shared his story with her, he ran the risk of her rejecting his love and her assuming he would treat her like all other Jews did. She could have said, "Get your own water, you Jew. Your people have been mean to us all our lives, and now you're only speaking to me because you need something." She could have said, "I'm sure you think you're somebody important. All you Jews think they're better than us."

Instead, she ran to town and told everyone she saw that they needed to see him too. As a result, many believed in Jesus as the Messiah.

The power of story

We have encountered this Jesus too. We've seen him address our sin with grace and forgiveness. And we understand that he is the Savior of the world!

It's important to know the value of our story. When we've put into practice the things Jesus modeled in response to racial and ethnic division, we will soon have our own stories of encounters with those outside our palace who belong in the stories of Jesus. We will experience the joy, life, and freedom of doing things Jesus's way, living free of bitterness, offense, and pride in the flesh.

I like using the phrase "if you only knew" when I can't describe how good something is. I'm thinking of those experiences when we don't have words to express what we know and what has happened. We know the only way for others to understand is to experience it for themselves, so we don't want to cheat them by using words that will minimize it.

This is how I feel about knowing Christ and being brought into relationship with God. This is also how I feel about the things Jesus did in response to race and how it frees us from bitterness, offense, and animosity. If we only knew how we all can make a difference from the least to the greatest. If we only knew, how much Jesus has given us through his teachings, life example, and sacrifice on the cross, we would have to run and tell everyone too.

If we only knew how freeing it is to not have to try to convince others of our views on the topic of race. Jesus's way is how we're supposed to love one another anyway, so we don't have to carry the burden of trying to change people's palace-formed thoughts. Our part is to simply do what Jesus did, and then our part is finished.

When Jesus died on the cross, he said, "It is finished" (John 19:30). How could he say that when the world had not heard of him, and all the nations had not yet received his goodness? Because his job was to be the living way into tomorrow.

Our job is not to force others, but to show by our example, to invite, and to share our stories. Start a big party among those who have kicked bitterness to the curb and chosen to live like Jesus. Work together to make things better where wrongs have been done (even if it takes a long time). Do it together, in love.

There's a risk of being rejected when we share the Good News of Jesus and of the joy and peace of God's way of handling the race topic. But there's also the potential of a great harvest like never before and a whole city welcoming Jesus like the Samaritans did. There are two ways to respond to the hope and joy that Jesus brings in every area of our lives:

1. We share the story of others out of obedience to the Great Commission, or
2. We become so filled with the joy of what God has done that it overflows from our lives like it did with the Samaritan woman.

I don't condemn any of us for taking the first option and serving Jesus because it is right, but if we can let go of offense and take time to see how wonderful he is, how awesome his plans are, and how much he could free every heart from bitterness, we could do the second option. We could respond like the Samaritan woman and find it hard to stop ourselves from running from city to city sharing the Good News.

Momentum, zeal, sacrifice, obedience, childlike and simple faith - these are the hidden riches of the stories of other ethnic groups and of those who are hungry for God, who do more with less because they hold nothing back from Jesus. It was the Samaritan woman who ran and told a whole city about Jesus. It was the Queen of Sheba who traveled at least 900 miles to hear the wisdom of Solomon. It was a recently freed demoniac who ran home and told everyone about Jesus. When people have had to live without the respect of others anyway, they are often quicker to give a wholehearted response to Jesus, his truth and his ways. We mustn't let our dignity be a bushel to the light. We can learn from Samaritans, like Jesus wanted us to.

When we think of the race conversation, have we begun to start saying "if you only knew," or is this topic still irritating you? It's hard to convince others about a message that has yet to convince you.

If we don't understand the value of our story, we are less likely to share it with others. The Samaritan woman experienced Jesus and was so deeply impacted that she had to go tell her story. She was not trained in doctrine. She had not followed Jesus and been made into a fisher of men like the apostles, but she shared the only thing she needed to know to get her community's attention, her story.

We don't have to become scholars in race history or get a theology degree before we start sharing our story of learning to love our neighbors and we enthusiastically spread the good news of how our hearts have been made better by Jesus. Sometimes, our intellectual pursuit and extra questions for Jesus are just covering the fear of man in our hearts.

What will my palace friends think of me?

What if they start treating me differently?

What if they misunderstand what I'm trying to say?

What if I suffer the loss of relationships, money, or position?

This was the case with Nicodemus who went by night to ask Jesus more questions. Jesus replied by telling this sincere Bible scholar that he needed to be "born again" or in essence, be willing to start over. In other words, he had to be willing to dump all his pride and be childlike in learning and pursuing Jesus. Nicodemus only had to be willing to follow Jesus like those lowly fishermen sitting at his feet if he really wanted to receive Him and know God. God resists the proud but gives grace to the humble according to James 4:6.

Don't be afraid to share your story. God will be with you and make more of you than you can make of yourself *if* you will trust him like a child. Nothing can replace responding to God with a childlike heart. Keep the joy of serving him. Being alive in God is greater than being calculated. John 17:21 oneness becomes reality when we share with others (from our hearts) what we've learned, both inside and outside our palace communities. It is far easier to respond to the story of a heart that is ablaze with God's love and truth, than to be faced with a cold list of rules about how we are supposed to love one another.

Address your palace community

Why are we still addressing race in this day and age? Because too many people calculated their responses to God's truth. They counted how much they would lose if they loved their neighbors. They thought about the embarrassment, rejection, and relationships they could lose if they made friends with "them."

Politicians calculated their likelihood of being re-elected if they were seen associating a little too much with "them." Pastors calculated a loss of members and tithes if their attempts to love those outside their palace were misunderstood. People thought about how they would look like sellouts if they were seen enjoying friendship with "them" a little too much. They knew how vicious the palace conversations could be and calculated that they would never want to be on the receiving end of those barbs.

James 1:2-3 says, "Dear brothers and sisters, when troubles of any kind come your way, consider it an opportunity for great joy. For you know that when your faith is tested, your endurance has a chance to grow."

Maybe that's why we need the poor, the Samaritan, those with real brokenness in their lives, and those delivered from drugs to show us how to be fishers of men without an instruction booklet. The Samaritan woman ran all around Samaria telling everyone *her story*. She brought the people of the city to Jesus because of how much her encounter with Jesus had impacted her.

We don't need a jaw-dropping story or to memorize books of the Bible (like the Pharisees) before you begin making a difference. Plan to learn all about the Word of God, but don't let that slow you down from sharing what you know like the blind man in John 9 who simply said, "I once was blind, but now I see."

Tell others about how the examples of Jesus' love and intentionality towards Samaritans has impacted you. Celebrate how your practice of these principles has made a difference in your life and in your relationship with others. Share your story in a way that people can hear you. Bring your light out from under the bushel. We share our stories, because there are people in our lives (and those we don't know) who will be moved by our story and not others.

If we calculate all the challenges and trials we may face, we'll probably find ourselves right back in our palaces, keeping a safe distance from the pain in the world. Remember, when Jesus started the Sermon on the Mount, he told us there would be challenges, persecutions, and trials. He told us to be ready to be gracious, meek, pure of heart, but still hungry to grow in his righteousness. So, we shouldn't be shocked or dismayed. There may be someone who needs to hear what we have to say.

There was a distinct moment in Matthew 10:5, when Jesus sent out the twelve apostles with instructions to not go to the Gentiles or the Samaritans. This was a moment of a clear assignment, where they were to make sure they made the call to repentance to their palace community of Jews first. In the palace, the inherent belief is that *they* need help more than we do. Blind thinking believes that *they* need to get right and then everything will be better. It may sound like:

- "If anybody needs to repent first, it is the Jews," thinks the Samaritan.
- "If anybody needs to repent first, it is the Samaritans," thinks the Jew.
- "If anybody needs to repent first, it is the Black people," thinks the White person.
- "If anybody needs to repent first, it is the White people," thinks the Black person.
- "If anybody needs to repent first, it is them, not us," think all of us.

Churches used to sing a hymn years ago that said, "Not my brother, not my sister, but it's me, oh Lord, standing in the need of prayer. It's me, it's me, it's me, oh Lord, standing in the need of prayer."

The prophet Isaiah exposed Israel's powerless fasting saying, "What good is fasting when you keep on fighting and quarreling? This kind of fasting will never get you anywhere with me" (Isaiah 58:4).

Jesus-thinking says to first take the speck out of our own eye, then we will see clearly. Jesus shows that all else is hypocritical.

"And why worry about a speck in your friend's eye when you have a log in your own? How can you think of saying to your friend, 'Let me help you get rid of that speck in your eye,' when you can't see past the log in your own eye? Hypocrite! First get rid of the log in your own eye; then you will see well enough to deal with the speck in your friend's eye." (Matthew 7:3-5)

Jesus sent the message of repentance to the children of Israel, his palace community, first. If we don't want to walk in blindness, then we must walk in humility. The first act of humility is to confess our blindness. Not only our own blindness, but we also offer that same opportunity to those in our palace worlds (those whom we influence), to repent (see a new way and change), for the Kingdom of Heaven is here.

God has a better way to handle race, and we have the opportunity and responsibility to change our ways and do it his way. Repentance, which is the opportunity to change, is a gift. We are encouraged to not harden our hearts when we hear his voice.

Jesus has not left us in the dark concerning how we are supposed to live in relation to "them." His desire for us to love our neighbors is clear. He modeled a life that was born out of God's heart, not man's bitterness. His responses to ethnic divisions are brilliant, but they aren't complicated. This is how Jesus walked. May we follow in his footsteps.

Use your platforms of influence

The Samaritan woman Jesus met at the well was likely known by many people in her town, and her story of broken marriages was probably known too. Her story of Jesus was powerful to her fellow Samaritans because they knew her (whether for positive or negative reasons).

If we've begun to relate to people outside our palace as Jesus did, we have something to invite people into. There are people in your palace community who will listen to you and maybe only you. They might consider these ways of Jesus only because they see you doing them. They might consider this conversation or even read this book only because you offer it to them. They connect with your palace world. They respect you, or they see themselves in you. They may never overcome their bitterness, hatred, or distance until they hear your story.

We can't make our story someone else's responsibility to share. Each of our stories has value. In fact, when it comes to the race topic, some of our palace community has been completely turned off by the conversation and has possibly given up hope. They're worn out from the constant division or the blindness they think the other group has. When they see you willing to walk in these ways, they can begin to see themselves doing it also.

Like Jesus, we must know that we're carrying Living Water. That is why we must be willing to share our stories. The story in John 4 with the Samaritans is rich because it's one of the only times where Jesus clearly said, "I am the Messiah." He didn't say it in a mysterious way. He said it directly. We are representatives of the Messiah. We are representatives of a love that is greater than the limitations of our ethnic groups and of the pains, issues, and offenses that have caused division between us and them.

If those who represent the light refuse to shine, then how can we blame the world for walking in darkness? As Jesus says, "No one lights a lamp and then puts it under a basket" (Matthew 5:15). If the darkness of division prevails in other communities, how can we claim to be angry at them if we won't walk in the light of Jesus's ways? How can we judge them if we have never sought a way to serve and be part of the solution? Jesus showed up in Samaria. He showed up in our worlds. He did not hide in the palace of heaven. He came to seek and save us, the lost.

Have you found yourself hidden in the safety of the palace? If so, how will you make your days count? King David prayed, "Teach me to number my days so that I may apply my heart to wisdom" (Psalm 90:12).

There will still be negative palace conversations, with condescending language, presumptions, and exaggerated stories. There are people saying they're done with that other ethnic group. Some may have gone as far as to threaten the lives of that other ethnic group because they believe their livelihood and posterity is under threat. Narratives can be dangerous. This darkness desperately needs the light that comes from those who will share a better story and do what Jesus did.

Chapter 13

Want What Jesus Wants

"After this I saw a vast crowd, too great to count, from every nation and tribe and people and language, standing in front of the throne and before the Lamb. They were clothed in white robes and held palm branches in their hands." Revelation 7:9

A better tomorrow today

Growing up in the 1980s, racial slurs were more commonly and openly used in America. I was born in St. Louis, Missouri. I remember coming home complaining to my parents that some of the White kids in our predominantly White neighborhood were calling me the n-word constantly as I walked home from school. My parents repeatedly reminded me of who I was and told me to not let words affect me.

Church was a different story. I remember gathering with our all-Black church as a child and hearing the older believers talk about how there would be no more racism in heaven, and that one day we would all be together before the throne of God. In Sunday School, we would sing, "Jesus loves the little children, all the children of the world—red and yellow, black and white—they are precious in his sight. Jesus loves the little children of the world." I wondered whether the Whites across town wanted the same thing and why race was an issue.

Preachers would quote Revelation 7:9 and talk about how "every nation, tribe, and tongue" would worship together before the throne of God one day. They would talk with a longing to one day live in a world that was free of prejudice, where they would be fully respected, and have fellowship and worship together with White believers and others without all of the division and hatred.

The preachers and believers said that great day would come when we all get to heaven. It was always, "One day things will change. One day things will be better." But the great day would be after we died or after Jesus returned. I believe what John saw in Revelations 7:9 is true, but I also discovered that Jesus taught his disciples to pray, "Your kingdom come, and your will be done on earth as it is in heaven" (Matthew 6:10).

As I came of age and grew in my understanding of the Bible, I was no longer looking for things to just be better in the sweet by and by (in heaven). I saw what Jesus prayed in John 17:20-23, and I became confident that I could pray for things to be better now. It was Jesus that wanted us to be one, so I was going to want what Jesus wanted and pray like Jesus prayed. God's Word helped me discover how to live and love others so that Jesus' prayers could become our reality. I saw that we could overcome the pain and ignorance that keeps people at odds with one another.

I love the picture of oneness in Revelations 7:9, but it is not just for tomorrow. The life Jesus modeled, things he taught, and intentionality behind his relationship to Samaritans makes it clear that Jesus wants oneness, and it is available today to whoever will do what Jesus did.

Walking as one is not just a nice option. It is part of the work and responsibility we have to represent Christ as his ambassadors in the world. Walking as one is not just something that we will "try" if we "get around to it" or "if it's convenient."

Walking as one is having a respect for Jesus, his sacrifice, and all our brothers and sisters in Christ. It is seeking to be cooperative and not just self-minded. It is celebrating the salvations, the victories, and the answered prayers of other believers and their churches too. It is refusing the temptation to bring division in the way we address topics concerning the church, the family of God, and its leaders. Walking as one was important to Jesus, so we will thrive in His plans in wonderful ways to the degree that being one is important to us too.

A secret to the harvest

Jesus wept over the city of Jerusalem because they had missed their opportunity to accurately reflect God's heart toward the world. Yet a city of Samaritans received Jesus. Why did a city of Samaritans respond to Jesus when Jerusalem did not? Pride and blindness.

In America, we must be careful of the same stumbling block. We have so much in this country. We have to be careful not to subtly get puffed up and begin looking down on others. It is possible to be thankful for the privileges, the freedom, and the many blessings we have been given by God in a way that makes us boast on God and not ourselves. Other countries and those with power, wealth and influence have the same opportunity.

Prayers are sometimes prayed that God would bring revival and move on the earth again as though he is not moving in other countries. Prideful thinking believes that God moving in other places is just primitive and the "real" move of God can only start with "us".

Second Chronicles 7:14 is a powerful call to repentance and humility. "Then if my people who are called by my name will humble themselves and pray and seek my face and turn from their wicked ways, I will hear from heaven and will forgive their sins and restore their land" (2 Chronicles 7:14).

God loves us and every other ethnic group. He is no more required to bless Americans than he was required to favor the Jews. If we want God to bless the United States of America, we would do well to humbly repent and pray not just for our palace group but for all of the people in this land, especially the body of Christ (see Daniel 9).

In sermons and books, when we hear the word "harvest" someone is usually talking about winning souls to follow Christ. How many times have we heard this exhortation and been challenged to not sit around waiting before we share the Good News? We quote John 4:35, where Jesus says, "Say not, 'Four months between planting and harvest.' But I say, wake up and look around. The fields are already ripe for harvest."

We say this so we remember our priority. Harvest brings visions of a time when droves of people come to know the beauty of Jesus for themselves. But we mustn't overlook the context that frames what Jesus was saying in John 4:35. Jesus had just finished speaking to the woman at the well and all the people of the city had come to hear Jesus for themselves. Jesus was surrounded by a harvest of Samaritans! He was surrounded by droves of "them," and they were all believing in Jesus for themselves.

It was in this setting that Jesus said to his disciples, "Wake up and look around. The fields are already ripe for harvest." They were in Samaria. They were surrounded by Samaritans when Jesus made this famous harvest statement. He was telling them the harvest was right in front of them, and it included those outside their palace walls.

Jesus is calling every follower to not stay settled in a palace setting of us-es and thems, but to go out and find the great harvest among the thems. When Jesus told his disciples, "Follow me, and I will make you fishers of men," I wonder whether they pictured non-Jews. I wonder whether they ever imagined they would be standing with Jesus surrounded by a sea of Samaritans who were acknowledging Jesus as Messiah and begging him to stay longer, which he did.

There is a harvest outside of our palaces, outside of our comfort zones. We see the harvest when we go among the thems and lift our eyes.

If the harvest we don't have to wait for is among those who are Samaritans to us, then we must be clear about who they are and where they are. Then we live a life like Jesus modeled, moving toward them to see healing and see God's plans happening on earth.

How had Jesus caused this great moment to happen in the first place? He had broken ethnic and cultural expectations by speaking to the Samaritan woman. One of the great testimonies that opens the hearts of others and draws them to Jesus is when they try to understand why a stranger would leave their comfortable and familiar relationships to care for them and bring the Good News. This testimony is part of what shows that we are sent by heaven.

The context of lifting our eyes to see the harvest is Jesus standing in Samaria surrounded by Samaritans, a group of people that the Jews would not have looked for to discover God's plans. What if this is a message to us all that we are prone to believing that God is going to move soon in our palace communities when he is actually calling us to come out of our palaces, our worlds of comfort, and find ourselves in spaces where we are around *them*? The command to "lift your eyes" is to see beyond our palace relationships.

God had a solution for the ethnic division and racial issues. The answer is in Jesus. His solution includes the Samaritans and not just the Samaritans receiving the message but the Samaritans being carriers of the message to be doers of his will and part of the family of God, just as much as any Jew would have the opportunity to be part of God's family. This vision is not for the faint of heart. We can hear our Father's desire. We can see that he wants us in the fields with him. Will we join him? Can you picture them loving well? Can you picture them carrying the good news throughout the earth? Can you picture them as your own beloved and cherished brothers and sisters in Christ? Can you see us and them sharing Communion together with our children, and our children's children for generations being faithful to Jesus and His dream until he returns? If you can't, pause for a minute and catch God's dream with all of your heart and zero fear and reluctance.

It's our turn to put the strategy of Jesus into practice, to step into the harvest by relating to "them" like Jesus related to the Samaritans.

The time is now

I was invited to California to share at a large conference about race and the Gospel. As I was preaching, I entered one of those moments where I was listening to my own thoughts and celebrating what I was hearing God say. I talked about how disappointing it was to see that generations of those who carried the Bible would not show the courage to reject the positions of racism that they held in America to support slavery and to support division.

I was also quick to say that I wondered whether I would have had the courage to stand. I hoped I would have had the courage to stand up if I were in their shoes, knowing that I could suffer, lose all my property, or even get lynched.

I remember standing there talking about how people misused Scripture to justify slavery in our country's history and had in Jesus's day too. Then it struck me that if those who twisted Scripture to support racism and division in America for more than 150 years could produce such pain, death, division, and domestic terrorism, what would happen if for the next 150 years we, the body of Christ, shared and practiced what Jesus really said?

God has taught me that complaining will never lead me to his plans and to never complain about anything that I wasn't willing to be used to change. I was to reject the temptation to point a finger at others or act like I would have shown more courage if I were living in a certain day when I can't prove that.

Instead, I have found it to be healthier to my soul to spend my time discovering what God is willing to do through me right now. What can God do through you? What will God do through you? What will happen in your world when you address race like Jesus did? What will happen when you go beyond the walls of your palace to love and know your neighbors?

In all the Scriptures, God has proved again and again that he can mightily use one person who is willing to say yes. We won't give an account for anyone else's behavior before God but our own.

Start doing what Jesus did today. The time for us to be one in Christ is now. The time for the harvest is now. The time for us to lift our eyes beyond our palace is now to see our opportunity to make a difference and "let your good deeds shine out for all to see, so that everyone will praise your heavenly Father" (Matthew 5:16).

It's the Kingdom of Heaven, God's way of doing things, his culture that beats all the division and pain of the world we live in. Reject comfort. Be intentional and be on assignment now. Share your story of how Jesus changed your heart concerning the race conversation and invite others into the journey.

What kind of yes are you willing to give Jesus?

"I pray that they will all be one, just as you and I are one—as you are in me, Father, and I am in you. And may they be in us so that the world will believe you sent me." (John 17:21)